SPAIN
art and tradition

P&M
EDICIONES

Published by: Ediciones Palacios y Museos
Editorial Coordination: Enric Balasch and Yolanda Ruiz
Translation from Spanish: NOVA Language Services

Cover design: Estudio JMD
Graphic Design, Layout and Cartography: Alejandro Gómez
Typeset: Lucam
Printed by: Artes Gráficas Palermo

ISBN: 978-84-8003-458-6
Legal deposit: M-25563-2014

Printed in Spain

CONTENTS

CITIES AND MONUMENTS

UNIQUE TOWNS AND VILLAGES

GASTRONOMY

TRADITIONAL FESTIVALS

TRADITIONAL FESTIVALS

CUSTOMS AND TRADITIONS

A CORUÑA
Cudillero
Luarca
OVIEDO
Llanes
Santillana del Mar
SANTANDER
BILBAO
SAN SEBASTIÁN
LUGO
PONTEVEDRA
OURENSE
Tui
LEÓN
PALENCIA
BURGOS
VITORIA
PAMPLONA
LOGROÑO
Sos del Rey Católico
Figueras
ZAMORA
VALLADOLID
SORIA
HUESCA
ZARAGOZA
LLEIDA
GIRONA
BARCELONA
TARRAGONA
La Granja de San Ildefonso
Pedraza
SALAMANCA
SEGOVIA
San Lorenzo de El Escorial
Sigüenza
Ciudad Rodrigo
La Alberca
ÁVILA
GUADALAJARA
TERUEL
Albarracín
Peñíscola
MADRID
Chinchón
Aranjuez
CUENCA
CASTELLÓ
PALMA DE MALLORCA
CÁCERES
Trujillo
Guadalupe
TOLEDO
VALENCIA
CIUDAD REAL
Mérida
BADAJOZ
ALBACETE
Almagro
ALACANT
CÓRDOBA
JAÉN
MURCIA
HUELVA
SEVILLA
GRANADA
Arcos de la Frontera
Ronda
Frigiliana
Nerja
MÁLAGA
ALMERÍA
CÁDIZ
LANZAROTE
TENERIFE
FUERTEVENTURA
LAS PALMAS

Piedra Monastery Nature Reserve

The land of Spain today, colonised by various cultures over its long history, retains a first-rate artistic heritage (second in the world only to Italy) that attracts both locals and visitors alike. What's more, the benign year-round climate at any time of year – especially true of the islands and on its Mediterranean coast – and a delicious and varied gastronomy, world famous festivals such as San Fermín, and countless monuments declared World Heritage Sites by UNESCO, have made Spain the fourth most-visited country in the world according to the World Tourism Organisation, with nearly 60 million foreign tourists travelling here every year.

In the last two decades, the organisations responsible for domestic tourism have sought to advertise the country's cultural assets overseas, and the results have been spectacular. For example, the Way of St. James began to be more actively promoted in 1993, as well as properly signposted and upgraded, and today thousands of foreign visitors travel it every year in search of the nature and art they can admire along every step of the way. In addition, Spain continues to be the destination of sun-and-sand tourism, especially in the summer months when millions of Spaniards and foreigners spend their holidays mainly on the Mediterranean coast, home to countless Blue Flag beaches. This rating, awarded by the European Foundation for Environmental Education, is given to beaches that comply with a series of requisites, such as water quality, safety (the presence of lifeguards), good general services and balanced environmental management systems.

Festivals have become another point of attraction, some drawing throngs of foreign visitors who come to Spain just to experience them. San Fermín, the *fallas* of Valencia, Holy Week in Andalusia, or Seville's April Fair top the list. Nor can the country's rich gastronomy be left out, heralded by great chefs such as Ferran Adrià, Juan Mari Arzak, Joan Roca, Carme Ruscalleda, Martín Berasategui, Pedro Subijana and Andoni Luis Aduriz, among many more, who have brought national cookery to the forefront of international gastronomy.

The tourists who visit Spain will leave with their bags packed with pleasant new experiences, fantastic photos and unique flavours, all brought together in this book to be recaptured at their leisure.

FROM PREHISTORIC TIMES TO THE AUTONOMOUS REGIONS

Spain, due to its geographical position in Southern Europe, has served as a cultural bridge since ancient times, having been colonised by various peoples who have all left their mark.

The great adventure known as Humanity began in Spain over 800,000 years ago in the Calabrian stage (the Pleistocene Epoch), as shown by the remains of *Homo antecessor* discovered at the Gran Dolina archaeological site (Atapuerca Mountains). The find has made the *Homo antecessor* the oldest hominid species found in Europe.

***Homo heidelbergensis*, Atapuerca**

Greek Colonisation

Between the 8th and 7th centuries BC, the Greeks disembarked in Spain, coming into contact with the local tribes settled on the Mediterranean coast which they called Iberians (from *Iber*, their name for the Ebro River). This is why the Greeks considered Iberia to be the coast of the Peninsula, as opposed to the interior, which they called Keltiké, as it was inhabited by Celtiberians.

Roman Conquest

Around the 6th century BC, the southern part of the peninsula fell under the control of Carthage; the new colonisers founded Qart Hadasht (Cartagena), which the Romans would later rename Carthago Nova. Rome saw the Carthaginian expansion in the peninsula as a threat to its interests, so they declared war on Carthage (the Punic Wars). After years of fighting, the Romans finally expelled the Carthaginians, vanquished the last pockets of resistance from the pre-Roman peoples (19 BC) and begun the Romanisation of the peninsula. Rome would impose its language, laws and religion upon Hispania, and three of the latter's sons would eventually become emperor: Trajan, Hadrian and Theodosius.

Conversion to Christianity

During the 3rd and 5th centuries, successive Germanic invasions (the Suebi, Alans, and Vandals) swept across the Pyrenees to sack the Peninsula, destroying Roman government infrastructure. The Visigoths, a branch of the Goths, came to Hispania as Roman allies, occupying Tarraconensis (*c.* 476) and installing their capital in Toledo. The conversion of Reccared to Christianity during the Third Council of Toledo (589) laid the foundation for the religious unity of the country. However, the constant warring between Visigoth families paved the way for the invasion of the Moors and their dominion over the peninsula for nearly eight centuries.

The *Lady of Elx*

The Invasion of Tariq ibn-Ziyad

The Visigoth king Wittiza appealed to the North African Moors to help defeat Roderic, so the troops of General Tariq, a Berber from Nafta, crossed the Pillars of Hercules, disembarked in the Peninsula and defeated Roderic in the Battle of Guadalete (711). By 716 the Moors had taken over nearly the entire southern half of the Peninsula, which they called Al-Andalus. In 929 Abd-ar-Rahman III established the Caliphate of Cordoba, which would become famous around the world.

Alfonso VI, Toledo

Alfonso VI, son of Ferdinand I, was stripped of his kingdom by his brother Sancho II, who considered himself to be his father's sole heir. Alfonso VI took refuge in the Moorish kingdom of Toledo, which he only left upon being named King of León, Castile, Galicia and Portugal. The rivalry between Castile and León during his regency for the control of the Peninsula would condition his hostility towards El Cid. In 1085, Alfonso VI took Toledo, where he died at the age of sixty-two.

The Decline of the Moors and the *Reconquista*

After the death of Almanzor (1002), the Al-Andalus soldier, politician and the warlord of the Cordoba Caliphate, the decline of the Moors began to set in due to infighting amongst the various families, which saw the caliphate dismembered into small kingdoms or *taifas*. Peace, however, never did reign in Saracen Spain. Asturians and Cantabrians, from their northern sanctuary, had stood up to the Moors from day one, and led by Pelayo they defeated the invaders in Asturias at the Battle of Covadonga (*c.* 722). The seizure of Toledo (1085), the campaigns led by *El Cid* (the Lord) and the conquest of Zaragoza would bring further momentum to the *Reconquista* or the Christian reconquest, which would spread even further at the onset of the 13th century. In 1212, the union of the Christian kingdoms in the Battle of Navas de Tolosa led to the defeat of the Moors and marked the beginning of the end of the *Reconquista*, culminating in the seizure of Granada (1492) by the Catholic Monarchs.

Templar Castle of Miravet

Replica of a caravel, Palos de la Frontera

Discovery of America

The support given to the Genovese navigator and cartographer Christopher Columbus by the Catholic Monarchs would set the stage for the discovery of America (12th October 1492). For Spain it would mean an enormous economic windfall: in just one hundred and fifty years, 17,000 tonnes of silver and 200 tonnes of gold were to dock at Spanish ports. Thanks to the riches brought from the Americas, art and architecture would flourish in Spain, while the shipping industry underwent an enormous expansion.

Charles I and the Revolt of the *Comuneros*

Charles I (1500-1558), son of Philip the Fair and Joanna the Mad, had united beneath his sceptre the possessions

Charles I of Spain, Titian

of the Austrian crown, the territories of the Spanish kingdoms and the Indies. In 1519, after the death of his grandfather Maximilian, he was crowned the emperor of the Holy Roman Empire in present-day Germany, thus becoming Charles V. The sinecures the King bestowed onto foreigners and the fears that matters in Germany would affect domestic affairs led to the Revolt of the *Comuneros*, the communities of Castile, as well as the Revolt of the Brotherhoods in Valencia and Majorca, the uprising against the Regency Council presided by Adrian of Utrecht (1520-1521), the future Pope Adrian VI. Imperial endeavours would drain its coffers and the King had to resort to financing from European bankers such as Fugger, Welser and Grimaldi.

The Counter-Reformation and the Spanish Armada

Philip II (1527-1598), son and heir of Charles I, in his attempt to counter the rise of Protestantism, made Spain the centre of the Counter-Reformation, thus consolidating his supremacy in the early years of his reign, especially after defeating the French in the Battles of St. Quentin (1557) and Gravelines (1558), the Ottomans at Lepanto (1571) and adding Portugal to his domain (1580). After 1558, Philip II had to face the revolt of the Low Countries, growing pressure from French Calvinists and the War of the Alpujarras (Granada). Lastly, a military coalition of England, France and Holland dealt him his first losses and forced his concessions: the fiasco of the Spanish Armada (1588) and having to permit an autonomous government in the Low Countries.

The Decline of the Spanish Empire

The reigns of Philip III and Philip IV marked the irrevocable decline of Spanish colonial power. The economy, buffeted by the high inflation inherited from the reign of Philip II, only grew worse due to the scarce demand

Charles III, the son of Philip V, succeeded his brother to the Spanish throne. His reign is considered as the one which most reflected the period of Enlightened Absolutism. He put in place a set of social reforms that laid the groundwork for the Industrial Revolution, expelled the Jesuits (1767) and began land reform. He waged two wars with Great Britain: in the first (1762) he lost Martinique, Florida and Sacramento, but received Louisiana in exchange; in the second (1779) he regained Florida and Minorca.

for agricultural products from the Americas and ever-rising prices, resulting in the downfall of industry. The expulsion of the Moriscos (Muslims who had been forced to convert to Christianity) in 1609 accentuated the precarious finances of the country, while Spain's participation in the Thirty Years' War (1618-1648) would end up sinking the economy for good. The Spanish defeat in the Battle of Rocroi (1643) forced it to recognise the independence of the Low Countries, and while the secessionist movement in Catalonia, known as the *Guerra de los Segadores* (the Reapers' War), was tamped down (1652), Spain ended up having to cede Roussillon to France in the Treaty of the Pyrenees (1659) and recognise the independence of Portugal through the Treaty of Lisbon (1668). Charles II, the last Hapsburg monarch, died without an heir, leaving the throne to Philip, grandson of Louis XIV of France, the Sun King. This set off the War of the Spanish Succession (1700-1715) which ended with the victory of the French pretender, who began the Bourbon dynasty under the name Philip V.

Charles III, Raphael Mengs

Charles III and the Enlightenment

Charles III (1716-1788) is considered to be the King of the Enlightenment, the intellectual movement that developed between the late 17th century and the French Revolution (1789). His ministers Esquilache and Grimaldi, and later Aranda, Floridablanca and Campomanes, would promote various reforms aimed at modernising society, although these would be rejected setting off the Esquilache Riots (1766). During the reign of Charles III, free trade with America was declared (1765) and thanks to the Peace of Versailles (1783), Spain received Florida and Minorca.

The French Occupation

Charles IV (1748-1819), due to his lack of experience in state affairs, handed over the reins to his favourite, Manuel Godoy, who he appointed Prime Minister (1792). Spain, allied with Britain, attacked France (1793), without much luck, and had to sign the Treaty of Basel (1795) and lost part of Hispaniola. Later Spain would join France, but its squadrons were defeated in the Battle of Trafalgar by Vice Admiral Nelson (1805). The Treaty of Fontainebleau (1807) stipulated that Portugal be shared between Spain and France, and in order to do so, Spain authorised French troops to pass through its territory, but Napoleon decided to occupy the country instead. Godoy was overwhelmed by the situation, resulting in the Mutiny of Aranjuez (1808). Charles IV abdicated in favour of his son, Ferdinand VII, but Napoleon forced him off the throne, naming his brother Joseph Bonaparte the Regent King of Spain. On 2nd May 1808, the people of Madrid rose up against French troops, setting off the Peninsular War, which ended with the defeat of Napoleon (1814).

The Carlist Wars

The Pragmatic Sanction (1789) by Ferdinand VII, which recognised women as having the right to the throne, nullified the royal aspirations of his brother Charles, who subsequently took to arms. Queen Maria Cristina, regent

***The Third of May 1808*, Goya**

Monument to the Cadiz Cortes

for her under-age daughter Isabella, the future Isabella II, sought the support of liberals and thus a civil war ensued between the Carlist (traditionalist) and liberal factions. Once the Carlist Wars had ended, Isabella II implemented policies that would consolidate the monarchy.

The First Spanish Republic

The turmoil that was unravelling Spain at the time culminated in the coup of Admiral Topete (1868), who was joined by Serrano and Prim, and the overthrow of Isabella II, who was exiled to Paris where she lived until her death in 1904. A provisional government, led by Francisco Serrano, convoked the *Cortes* ("the constituent assembly"), which opted to enact a liberal Constitution (1869) under a monarchical regime. Amadeo of Savoy (Amadeo I of Spain) was crowned king, but the fighting between supporters of the Republic, Carlists, and monarchists forced him to abdicate (1873) and flee to Lisbon, from where he returned to his native Turin (Italy) with his wife and three children. At that point the *Cortes* proclaimed the First Spanish Republic (11th February 1873).

Restoration of the Monarchy

After the coup by Martínez Campos (1874), Alfonso XII, the son of Isabella II, was proclaimed king. Alfonso enacted a conservative Constitution (1876) and upon his death his wife Maria Cristina became regent, who would see the lights fade on the remnants of the Spanish colonial empire. During the reign of Alfonso XIII (1902-1931) new political forces came on the scene (Republicans and Socialists), as did the first unions (CNT and UGT). To calm tempers, Antonio Maura, President of the Council of Ministers, attempted to make some reforms, but the 1909 revolt in Barcelona (the *Setmana Tràgica* or Tragic Week), touched off by the dispatching of troop reserves to Africa, would ruin his plans.

Alfonso XIII

Alfonso XIII, the posthumous son of Alfonso XII, was proclaimed king upon his birth. During his reign, he witnessed the stripping of the last remnants of the Spanish colonial empire, although he did consolidate the occupation of Morocco. He lent support to the dictatorship of Primo de Rivera (1923-1930), but after the triumph of the Republic in the 1931 municipal elections he was forced to leave the country.

World War I

Spain remained neutral during the First World War and thus enjoyed a certain economic windfall thanks to its coal exports, but this would only worsen tensions between the workers and the capitalist class. Adding to the flames of instability (1917-1923) were peasant revolts, Army discontent, the rebellion of the Catalan Parliament and the Battle of Annual (1921), the disastrous defeat of Spanish troops in the Rif at the hand of Berber combatants. The military coup by Primo de Rivera, Captain-General of Catalonia, would salvage the monarchy, but in exchange for installing him as dictator.

The Second Spanish Republic

The municipal elections of 1931 were won by the Republicans and on 14th April the Second Republic was proclaimed, presided by Niceto Alcalá Zamora. A new Constitution was voted in (1931), Catalonia was given a statute of autonomy, and agrarian reform was undertaken (1932), but several revolutionary flare-ups led to a rightward turn in the 1933 elections, when the conservative parties gained the majority. The uprisings in Catalonia and Asturias were put down (1934) and in the 1936 elections, the left-leaning parties, grouped together into the Popular Front, emerged victorious. The new Republican government was led by Manuel Azaña, but on 18th July of the same year General Francisco Franco would take up arms and the Civil War would begin (1936-1939).

Juan Carlos I of Spain

From the Franco Dictatorship to Democracy

An Organic Law (1966) would permit the designation of Juan Carlos de Borbón as the successor to General Franco, and upon the death of the dictator (20th November 1975), he was proclaimed king as Juan Carlos I. The king, along with Adolfo Suárez, helped usher in the democratic process. Political parties were legalised in 1976, and after the general legislative elections of June 1977, democracy was officially established. In 1978 a Constitution was approved which recognised the system of autonomous regions as way of decentralising the government.

The Abdication of Juan Carlos I

After a 39-year reign, on 2nd June 2014 King Juan Carlos announced his abdication of the throne and on 19th June, his son, Prince Felipe de Borbón, was proclaimed King of Spain under the title Felipe VI.

Madrid, 22/05/04. The Prince and Princess of Asturias, Felipe de Borbón and Letizia Ortiz, honour the tradition of offering the bride's bouquet to the Virgin of Atocha after their marriage in Almudena Cathedral.

Pamplona City Hall

CITIES AND MONUMENTS

CITY WALLS

The walls of Ávila rank among the most important medieval structures still standing in Spain due to the size of their perimeter and their excellent state of repair.

The first stone of the walls was laid by the Romans, but they reached their maximum splendour in the Middle Ages. At the end of the 11th century, Alfonso VI of Castile, after his conquest of Toledo (1085), ordered Count Raymond of Burgundy to repopulate the so-called "no-man's land" and fortify the cities of Segovia, Salamanca and Ávila.

The current walls, according to traditional historiography, were built in nine years between 1090 and 1099, although recent studies have suggested this time period was too short due to the complexity of the construction. Count Raymond of Burgundy, a French noble who brought the Burgundy dynasty to León and Castile through his marriage to Alfonso VI's daughter, Princess Urraca of León, commissioned the building of the walls to Casandro Romano and Florín de Pituenga (modern historians are unconvinced of the latter's involvement), who completed a perimeter of just over 2.5 km extending over 33 hectares, with 9 gates, 88 keeps and 2,500 merlons. The walls were built from the stones of the former Roman wall, a necropolis from the same epoch, and the remains of the Visigoth wall, as well as blocks of grey and black granite, brick, mortar and lime. Twelve metres high and three metres thick, the Walls of Ávila were considered to be impregnable for centuries, right up to the invention of artillery.

The importance of this military fortification, the only one of its size in Europe, led to its declaration as a World Heritage Site by UNESCO in 1985. The walls' fine state of repair is thanks to several restorations carried out over the centuries.

The Tower Keep

The city of Ávila during its festivals

BASILICA OF THE SAGRADA FAMÍLIA

The Temple Expiatori de la Sagrada Família sits atop the list of Spain's most visited sights, with three million, two hundred thousand tourists who come to Barcelona each year to admire the construction of the last "cathedral in Europe".

Built in the style of the old Gothic cathedrals, the first stone of the Sagrada Família was laid on 19th March 1882 by Francisco de Paula del Villar, and when the work eventually finishes on this grand basilica, it will have taken much longer than a century to complete, just like the great medieval cathedrals of Europe.

From the end of 1883 until his death in 1926, the man in charge of the project was the architect Antoni Gaudí. When he joined the project, he brought a new dimension to the Sagrada Família, whose neo-Gothic lines at the time came to be inspired by the Catalan *Modernisme* architectural style that Gaudí had been developing from his early days. The result of this change in orientation is fascinating, as can be seen in the spires, growing ever more slender as they rise and topped by ceramic pinnacles and crosses. The towers of the Sagrada Família, now a symbol of the city of Barcelona, neatly encapsulate the avant-

The Nativity Façade

The Passion Façade

garde and surrealist features of Antoni Gaudí's architecture. The parts of the Sagrada Família that Gaudí had completed, the Nativity Façade and the Crypt, were declared a World Heritage Site by UNESCO (2005). On 7th November 2010, Pope Benedict XVI consecrated the church and proclaimed it a Basilica in a ceremony that drew thousands of Europeans to Barcelona. From that moment on, the international fame of the Sagrada Família has grown spectacularly, with the number of visitors multiplying to reach the figure mentioned above. The crypt contains the tomb of the architect, Antoni Gaudí, who died in Barcelona, run over by a tram.

Columns of the Transept

PARK GÜELL

Set in the hills of Barcelona, on the southern slopes of Carmel Mountain, Park Güell was founded upon an initiative of the Catalan industrialist Eusebi Güell.

Bench in the shape of a dragon's tail

Architect Antoni Gaudí was commissioned with the construction of Park Güell by his close friend Eusebi Güell, and the leading figure in Catalan *Modernisme*, as with many others of his works, left behind his distinctive touch. The initial concept behind the project, carried out between 1900 and 1914, was to design sixty individual housing plots arranged in a sort of "garden city", as it was defined at the time, where each would enjoy a view overlooking Barcelona. Eusebi Güell greatly admired the English landscaped garden, designed to humanise industrial cities, so he hired Gaudí to build him a residential villa immersed in the lush vegetation of the area. However, the plan went wrong, as only two plots were sold (Gaudí lived in one until moving his studio into the Sagrada Família). The park, declared a World Heritage Site, has some rather curious fea-

The Salamander Fountain

Staircase and Hypostyle Room

tures, such as its enormous ceramic bench symbolising a dragon's tail, the Salamander fountain presiding over the entrance, the impressive Hypostyle Room decorated with ceiling roses composed of *trencadís* (small multi-colour ceramic fragments), and the oval-shaped pavilions at the entrance forming part of the park enclosure. It is crowned by a 10-metre high tower covered in blue and white tiles and capped by a red and white topped mushroom, a fly agaric *(Amanita muscaria)*. The failure of the Park Güell project led to it being opened to the public in 1926.

CATALAN *MODERNISME* ARCHITECTURE

Barcelona was among the great European capitals of *Modernisme*, a turn-of-the-century artistic movement that has any number of names according to the country where it occurred: *Art Nouveau, Sezessione, Jugendstil, Floreale, Liberty*, etc. Passeig de Gràcia, one of the city's main boulevards, features an ample repertoire of *Modernista* houses built by some of the best architects of their time: Antoni Gaudí, Puig i Cadafalch and Domènech i Montaner to name a few. Nevertheless, there are emblematic structures built in the Modernista style located elsewhere in the city, such as the Sagrada Família, Hospital of the Holy Cross and St. Paul, the *Casa de Les Punxes* (House of Spikes), Park Güell and the *Palau de la Música* (the Palace of Music).

In respect to architecture, Catalan *Modernisme* arose in the late 19th century out of the urge of some artists to make a break with the traditional criteria and formalism of the time that restricted their ideas. They opted for a new aesthetic ideal that was more in tune with the ways of thinking and technological advances of the 20th century. Experts consider this movement to be the logical outcome of the Industrial Revolution and the social and technological advances of the day which were changing the way society had always lived and thought.

Catalan *Modernisme* was led by the Barcelona School, where nearly all the architects working in Catalonia in the early 20th century were trained, and they would set the trends for the movement in the rest of Spain. The fame garnered by these architects led to commissions in other regions so their work is dotted across Spain, with good examples found in the Jesuit Church of Gijón by Jujol and El Capricho (the Whim) in Comillas, built by Gaudí. However, Catalan *Modernisme* lacks a common denominator

***Palau de la Música*, Domènech i Montaner**

Casa Milà, Gaudí

for it to be described as an organised movement. This would explain why figures such as Domènech i Montaner, Gaudí, Puig i Cadafalch, Joan Rubió, Jujol and Rafael Masó, among others, produced such a wide variety of buildings architecturally-speaking. Coherence within Catalan *Modernisme*, beyond its architecture and art must be found in the cultural environment that Barcelona was experiencing at the time, especially among the bourgeoisie involved in commerce and industry. *Modernisme* broke away from traditional industrial architecture by adding new aesthetic lines that revolutionised façades and the materials used to build them.

THE PICASSO MUSEUM

Pablo Picasso, perhaps the most universal Spanish painter of all time, resided in Barcelona for years and the city has honoured him with a grand museum.

In 1895, at the age of fourteen, Pablo Picasso and his family moved to Barcelona into a boarding house on Passeig de Isabel II, and shortly afterwards he passed the entrance exam at La Llotja, the School of Fine Arts. After a period in Paris, he returned to Barcelona and began work at the studio of Ángel Fernández de Soto, beginning what was to be called his Blue Period. He and Fernández de Soto often frequented the city's brothels, and his impressions were embodied in a series of erotic drawings, among them *Self-portrait with Reclining Nude* and *La Macarra (The Gangster's Moll)*, both of which can be seen at the Picasso Museum of Barcelona.

The Picasso Museum of Barcelona, sprawling over five palaces on Montcada Street built between the 13th and 14th centuries, displays some of the artist's finest works. In 1968, after the death of Sabartés, Picasso donated 58 paintings to the museum from his series of *Las Meninas* (1957), along with the *Portrait of Sabartés*, which he had painted in 1901, and promised to donate to the museum an engraving of all the works he would dedicate to his friend in the future. In 1970 Picasso made a second donation consisting of 921 works in different styles. In 1982, his widow, Jacqueline Roque, presented the museum with over 40 ceramic pieces, and the following year, his heirs donated 117 engravings and the Picasso-Raventós Foundation has given the museum the painting of *The Dead Woman* (1903).

The Picasso Museum

The Picasso Museum

THE RAMBLA

The Rambla of Barcelona, also called Les Rambles, is among the most famous boulevards in all Europe, drawing thousands of tourists every year.

Beneath a long green blanket formed by the tops of its plane trees, this boulevard unites Plaça Catalunya, the city's hub of activity, and the old port. At the head of the Rambla stands its most famous fountain, Canaletes, whose waters used to come from the Montcada spring, but now are piped directly from the city water supply. It is popularly said that outsiders who drink its water will one day return to Barcelona.

The Rambla is famous for the throngs of people strolling along at any time, day or night, especially when a cruise ship has docked at the nearby port. This popular boulevard, flanked by nineteenth century buildings (the Boqueria, Liceu Opera House, the Royal Academy of Sciences, the Hotel Oriente, the Masò Pharmacy, Casa Figueres, etc.), features a ceramic mosaic by the painter Joan Miró set among its paving stones and is dotted with flower stalls, newspaper stands, street performers, bars, restaurants, hotels, two prestigious music shops and countless other establishments. At the end stands the Convent of St. Monica, founded in 1619 by the Order of Augustinian Recollects and saved from the ecclesiastical confiscations of 1835 of Álvarez Mendizábal. The convent has since been converted into Arts Santa Mònica, an exhibition hall inaugurated in 1988 with a retrospective on surrealism in Catalonia. A bit further down the Rambla is the Wallace Fountain whose four caryatids hold up a dome symbolising peace among nations.

The Rambla

Street performers

The fountain, by the French sculptor Charles Auguste Lebourg, was given to the city by Sir Richard Wallace, the illegitimate son of Richard Seymour, a famous English multimillionaire and art collector.

Majestically rising (60 metres high) at the edge of the old port in the Portal de la Pau (the Peace Gate) is a monument to Christopher Columbus by the architect Gaietà Buïgues for the Barcelona World's Fair, which was opened on 8th June 1888. The column, which contains a small lift, is topped by a 7-metre tall statue of the Admiral sculpted by Rafael Atché, whose characteristic naturalist style was honed in the workshops of the brothers Agapito and Venancio Vallmitjana where he trained and worked. Near the monument to Columbus stands a small monolith that honours the 49 US marines who lost their lives on the morning of Monday, 17th January 1977, when their launch ran into a cargo ship.

The Canaletes Fountain

THE BOQUERIA MARKET

The Boqueria Market, also called Sant Josep, began in 1840 when an area was set aside so peasants from the nearby farming region of El Prat could have a place to sell their products.

The current location of the market was occupied many years ago by the Convent of St. Joseph (Josep in Catalan) founded by the Order of the Barefoot Carmelites (in Catalan called *josepets* because they spread the cult of St. Joseph along with Teresa of Ávila). The convent, much like the other religious buildings along the Rambla, was sacked and burned by anticlerical groups during the Barcelona riots of 1835. After the fire it was abandoned, and the site was expropriated by the city government, who built the market of the Boqueria in its place. There are more than 300 stalls spread over its 2,583 m^2, some currently run by Japanese, Greek and Italian immigrants, lending it an ethnic touch.

The industrial-style architecture of the market's roof was put up in 1914, although it was not until just a few years ago that the neoclassical colonnade of Sant Josep Square was restored, which had been built by the master builder Josep Más in 1850. Inside the market there is a constant hustle and bustle from the throngs of shoppers and tourists wandering its aisles to admire the stalls (*parades* in Catalan) selling vegetables, meats, cold cuts, and above all the fishmongers who shout out to possible customers. The Boqueria is a market drawing the admiration of locals and foreigners alike, not to mention great chefs such as Ferran Adrià and Thomasina Miers of the Wahaka restaurant (London).

One of the most interesting market stalls in the Boqueria is Petràs Fruits del Bosc, selling dozens of different types of fresh and dried mushrooms, all displayed in wicker baskets. Right off the entrance is

Main entrance

Fishmonger

The Petràs Fruits del Bosc mushroom stand

the popular bar Pinotxo, which attracts hundreds of diners every day with its market cuisine and many specialities. Cooked over a cramped stove, this temple of Mediterranean cuisine serves up some rather scrumptious dishes, such as sautéed baby squid and white beans, chick peas and black sausage, monkfish in vermouth, potatoes and spider crab, or just some mouth-watering anchovies.

PORT VELL

The old port, presided over by the monument to Christopher Columbus, was opened to the public during the 1992 Olympics.

Port Vell, the old port of Barcelona, was founded at the same time as the city, occupying an inlet located between a small peninsula jutting off Montjuïc Mountain and the mouth of the Llobregat River. Little by little the city and its port began to gain importance, and in 1378 Peter IV of Aragon finished the construction of the *Drassanes Reials* (the Royal Shipyards), a large Gothic complex intended for the building of galleys for the king of Aragon's royal fleet. In 1423, twelve galleys at these shipyards were completed at the same time, a testament to its importance, and in 1571 John of Austria's royal galley was built here, the flagship of the Battle of Lepanto. Since 1941, the royal shipyards have been home to the Barcelona Maritime Museum, which exhibits its collections of amphorae, anchors, cannon, figureheads, etc., and a life-size replica (60 metres long) of the royal galley of John of Austria.

Golondrina docked at the Drassanes pier

Port Vell and the Golondrinas

In 1477, under the reign of John II of Aragon, the first stone was set in what is now known as *Port Vell* (the old port), which grew over the centuries into the port complex that it is today, 829 hectares with over 20 kilometres of piers and 35 terminals: 3 maritime terminals for ferry docking, 7 international terminals for cruise ships (which carry nearly 3 million passengers per year), 4 for containers, 2 for vehicles, 1 for fruit, 2 for speciality cargo (cacao, coffee and non-ferrous metals), 1 refrigerated terminal, 9 for liquids in bulk and 6 for solids. The various terminals are served by 45 cranes and 9 tugboats. These facilities situate the Port of Barcelona in third place in the country's overall ranking in terms of container traffic (two million a year).

Overlooking the old port is the Columbus Monument and the former customs house. Next to the customs house is the famous *Moll de les Drassanes* (the Shipyard Pier), also called the Pier of the *Golondrinas*, after the shallow draught tourist boats that ply the waters inside the port and a short way up the Barcelona coastline. These boats came into service in 1888 for the first Barcelona World's Fair, and in those days they had capacity for twenty passengers and were steam powered.

GUGGENHEIM MUSEUM

Bilbao, on the banks of the Nervión River, shows visitors its most avant-garde facet at the Guggenheim Museum.

The museum, part of the Solomon Robert Guggenheim Foundation created in 1937 to promote Modern Art, is considered one of the best works of the Canadian architect Frank Owen Gehry. Gehry designed the building to have slightly twisted curvilinear forms and he clad it in limestone, titanium panels and enormous windows so natural light could flood the interior, thus allowing visitors to admire the artwork without having the colours altered by the effects of artificial lighting. Philip Johnson, a prestigious American architect, defined the Guggenheim Museum Bilbao as "the greatest building of our time".

The museum entrance is guarded by the famous *Puppy*, a work by the American artist Jeff Koons, the first to use an advertising company to promote his art, which stands out for being monumentally "kitsch".

Main entrance and *Puppy*

The Guggenheim Museum, rear view

Maman, Louise Bourgeois

Some of the most important pieces of the 20th century can be found right upon entering the building. Richard Serra's *The Matter of Time* became part of the museum's permanent collection in 2005, an installation of seven monumental sculptures which incorporates an earlier work, *Snake*, made for the inauguration of the Guggenheim. There are also temporary exhibitions of work from previous epochs, such as several Michelangelo drawings, Hermitage Museum paintings, Dürer engravings, and objects from the Kunsthistorisches of Vienna.

CATHEDRAL OF ST. MARY MAJOR

After Ferdinand I was crowned in León, Burgos became the capital of the Kingdom of Castile and enjoyed its period of greatest economic splendour, which accounts for the proliferation of so many religious buildings.

The finest example of the grand medieval buildings of Burgos is its French Gothic cathedral devoted to St. Mary Major, begun in 1221 and concluded in 1260. A meeting point for pilgrims during the Middle Ages on their way to Compostela to kneel before the tomb of St. James the Apostle, the cathedral underwent certain modifications in the 15th and 16th centuries, which provided it with the impressive needles on the main façade, the Chapel of the Constables and the *cimborrio*, its remarkable octagonal tower. In the 17th century, the sacristy and the Chapel of St. Thecla were erected and the portals on the main façade were changed.

The exterior features the façade of St. Mary, whose portal is composed of three ogive arches containing three doors: the Royal or Forgiveness Gate (in the centre), and those of the Immaculate Conception and the Assumption (to the sides). There is fascinating iconography devoted to the Virgin on the 13th-century portal. Inside the church, it is well worth mentioning the Main Chapel, composed of three sections and ribbed arches presided over by a Renaissance-style

North Façade, Portal of St. Mary

altarpiece (15th century), the work of the brothers Rodrigo and Martín de la Haya. The altarpiece contains an image of St. Mary Major (15th century), painted in the Flemish-Gothic style. In the presbytery, there are several Gothic tombs, among them John of Castile, the son of Alfonso X the Wise. At the foot of the main nave is the *Papamoscas* (the Flycatcher), an 18th-century clock figure who marks the hours by striking a bell with his right arm at the same time he opens his mouth. In the centre of the same nave is

Sacrament Façade

Pinnacles

the choir, featuring 103 Renaissance-era walnut stalls made by the master wood carver Felipe Bigarny. The main chapels worth noting include the Chapel of the Constables (15th century), the Pantheon of Pedro Fernández de Velasco and Menecía de Mendoza, with a 14th-century altarpiece by Diego de Siloé and Felipe Bigarny, and the tombs made of Carrara marble.

THE ROMAN THEATRE AND MUSEUM

Cartagena, Qart Hadasht for the Carthaginians, which the Romans renamed Carthago Nova, preserves its past in the form of a theatre and a collection of sculptures on display in its modern museum.

The Roman theatre of Cartagena is among the greatest legacies that Roman culture left in Hispania. Dating from the epoch of Emperor Augustus, between 5 and 1 BC, the structure belongs to the city's period of greatest growth after being declared a colony as *Urbs Iulia Nova Carthago*. Discovered in 1988 by Dr Sebastián Ramallo, a professor at the University of Murcia, during one of his archaeological digs, the theatre can seat up to 7,000 spectators and was still in use until the 3rd century. Afterwards it was abandoned and various buildings were erected on top of it. Due to its importance, on 21st January 1999 the theatre was designated a Cultural Heritage Site in the Monument category.

***Apollo Citharede* (1st century BC)**

The theatre structure is noteworthy for its columns carved out of red travertine *(lapis tiburtinos)*, or "Tivoli stone", found in the Mula quarries of Murcia, while the richly decorated sculptures of white marble quarried in Mount Pentelicus (Greece) or Carrara (Italy) were sculpted in the Imperial workshops in Rome. Once finished, the sculptures were transported by sea to Carthago Nova. According to the engravings found on the lintels, the theatre is dedicated to Lucius and Gaius Caesar, the grandsons of Octavius Augustus. The old Byzantine quarter and the theatre were buried beneath the Cathedral of Cartagena in the 13th century, whose walls bear remains from various epochs. Thanks to its excellent restoration, the theatre can shine once again. The reconstruction has integrated the museum and theatre into a single unit, and only upon completing a tour through the museum can the Roman theatre be accessed.

Designed by Rafael Moneo, the entrance lies opposite the City Hall and consists of two clearly defined buildings joined by an underground corridor that also connects the Palace of Pascual de Riquelme and an archaeological corridor below the Church of St. Mary the Old. The palace façade features a coat of arms carved in white

Cavea of the Roman theatre

The *Eagle of Jupiter* (1st century BC)

marble with the seal of the Garre family (a tree and a rampant lion) and the Garcias of Cáceres (three herons whose wings unfold over a castle).

The museum contains an interesting collection of items found during the theatre excavation. The tour begins along a corridor which explains the evolution of the theatre site from the 1st to the 21st centuries. Several panels, videos and models are used to show how the theatre was built in accordance with the standards of Marcus Vitruvius (1st century BC), author of *De Architectura*. The glass cases are packed with objects uncovered during the various excavations.

THE MOSQUE

This masterpiece of Islamic art, due to its fine state of repair and architecture, was declared a World Heritage Site by UNESCO.

In 785, the first stone of this monumental mosque was lain atop the site of the former Visigoth basilica of St. Vincent the Martyr (remains of which were found after excavations in 1940). Certain alterations were made during the Caliphate of Cordoba to enlarge the temple area. In 1238, after the reconquest of Cordoba, the mosque was consecrated as a Catholic cathedral, ordaining Lope de Fitero as its first bishop. In 1523 construction began on the Renaissance-style basilica in the core of the Islamic building.

The 23,400 m^2 Cordoba Mosque was the second largest of its time after the Grand Mosque in Mecca (today Saudi Arabia). Next to the Gate of Forgiveness, the main entrance, is the Courtyard *(sahn)* of the Orange Trees; the faithful used it in the era of the caliphate to perform their ablutions in the fountains *(sabil)*. The Gate of the Palm Trees provides access to the interior of the mosque, which contains 1,300 marble, jasper and granite columns that uphold 365 horseshoe arches. The richly decorated marble *mihrab* (a niche indicating where those praying should face) has multi-coloured stucco and Byzantine mosaics, which stand out over the gold and bronze background. Several naves designed by Hernán Ruiz were built in the 16th century after the mosque was reconverted into a Christian basilica, which would alter the original design of the temple.

The bell tower, the former minaret

Interior of the Mosque

THE ALHAMBRA

The capital of the Zirid Kingdom during the 11th century and the Nasrid Kingdom between the 13th and 15th centuries, Granada is home to the Alhambra, the most important example of Islamic art in Europe.

The Alhambra (from *al-hambra*, the Arabic word for red and called al-qala al-Hambra, "the Red Fortress" by the Arabs of Al-Andalus), is a palatial compound and fortress considered to be the masterpiece of Islamic art on the Iberian Peninsula and ranks among the most visited sights in Spain. Its magical location atop the Medina Ridge overlooking the Darro River lends a unique dimension to its perfect natural and architectural unity. This palatial precinct was used as the residence of the Nasrid dynasty, the last Moor dynasty of the Kingdom of Granada, which governed between 1238 and 1492.

The general shape of the palatial city is quite irregular: its maximum length and width measuring 740 and 220 metres respectively; the surrounding walls contain 25 keeps (the oldest being the tower keep) and five main gates: The Gate of *Xerea* or Justice, Gate of the Seven Floors, Gate of Arms, Gate of the Citadel and Gate of the Peaks. The best of the overall site, which appears to be a solid fortress with its walls and horseshoe-arched gates when seen from the outside, are the Nasrid palaces, which include the Palace of Comares and Courtyard of the Lions. The extremely fine quality of the architecture can be seen in its ornamentation, especially evident in the perfectly square Chamber of the Ambassadors (14th century), 11 metres per side and 18 metres high; the floor originally had marble slabs (today it is clay), and in the centre there is a square with the name Allah set in ceramic tile. Another example is the Hall of the Abencerrajes,

Arch with decorative plastering

The Alhambra, from the St. Nicholas viewing point

the Sultan's alcove, whose windowless walls are decorated in stucco and a tile dado (16th century) made in Seville, perhaps in the Triana district. The dome of the Abencerrajes is a richly ornamented display of *muqarnas*, a stalactite ceiling whose many colours are reflected in the fountain occupying the centre of the room. It is said that the central fountain of this room was the site where the members of a Granada family, the Abencerrajes, were executed in the struggle to control the kingdom.

However, the absolute height of Nasrid art can be found in the Courtyard of the Lions (14th century), which was built on the order of Mohammed V, the son of Yusuf I, who commissioned its design to Abén Cecid. Trapezoidal in shape, the courtyard is flanked by 124 white marble columns from the Macael quarries of Almeria, topped by cubic capitals engraved with various inscriptions. The gallery features a wooden coffered ceiling with interlaced laths. The delicate wood columns are grouped in twos, threes and even fours in order to uphold the filigree arches. The gallery leads in different directions to the private rooms and quarters of the sultan and his harem. Water is channelled through four of the rooms (the four join into one in the centre) to represent the four rivers of Paradise, a symbol that also appears in the cloisters of many Christian monasteries. In the middle of the courtyard is a remarkable fountain (14th century) composed of twelve lions - also carved in Macael marble – which bears the zodiac sign of Leo, fitting its astrologically–based symbolism. Tradition has it that this fountain once belonged to a palace of a Jew. This hypothesis is based on the fact that the lions might also symbolise the twelve tribes of Israel which uphold the Sea of Galilee, which would correspond to the twelve bulls that upheld the fountain in the palace of Solomon. On the edge of the basin there is a prayer inscription from Ibn Zamrak that reads: "Blessed be he who gave the Imam Mohammad ideas that adorned by their beauty all other villas". The courtyard has undergone great transformations over the passage of time, according to the records which have been kept. In 1537, it is known that various master builders worked on its decoration, and in 1552, Count Tendilla ordered some work to be carried out "that matched the Moorish originals" so as to "be in keeping with the old". In 1590 a fire

Courtyard of the Lions

Round arch with calligraphy and Arabesque motifs

Palace of Charles V

considerably damaged the Courtyard of the Lions and some locks disappeared from the doors.

The Alhambra precinct also contains the palace of King Charles V of Germany, or Charles I of Spain. The palace rises in the heart of the Moorish Alhambra, at one end of the luxurious courtyard of the Arrayanes, which was why it was necessary to demolish a pavilion opposite the Tower of Comares. The two-floor building was designed according to the canons of Roman architecture. The Tuscan-style ground floor contains pilasters decorated with great bronze rings, while the top floor, in the Ionic design, has pilasters alternating with lintel openings. The Palace of Charles V is home to the Fine Arts Museum of Granada, the city's most important painting collection featuring works by Alonso Cano and Sánchez Cotán, among others.

The Alhambra from the Albaicín

TIMANFAYA NATIONAL PARK

Lanzarote, the northernmost of the Canary Islands, seduces its visitors with the magic of its many colours.

The abrupt, bare landscapes of Timanfaya National Park (in the Yaiza and Tinajo municipalities) figure among the main attractions of Lanzarote (the park is visited by one and a half million people per year). The volcanic eruptions, which devasted much of the island between 1730 and 1736, formed the craters, lava flows and fields of ash seen in this park, where there are no trees and scarcely any vegetation or water. This desert landscape opens up before the eyes of its visitors, who can admire its unique formations, colours that change according to the position of the sun, and the incredible textures that are fruit of a geological process lasting thousands of years. Of the 25 volcanoes found in the park, the most important are Mount Rajada, the Mountains of Fire and the Caldera of *Corazoncillo* (the Little Heart).

Nevertheless, hidden amidst the arid landscape of Timanfaya are lichen formations, endemic plants such as the *salado blanco (Aizoon hispanicum)*, a type of stone plant, and several vertebrate species, such as

An excursion on camel back

Geyser

the Canary shrew *(Crocidura canariensis)* and the Haria lizard *(Gallota atlantica)*, not to mention several species of migratory birds which colonise the park in spring and autumn, and other nesting birds such as the Barbary partridge *(Alectoris barbara)*, common kestrel *(Falco tinnunculus)* and the common barn owl *(Tyto alba)*.

The small and deeply traditional villages that surround Timanfaya National Park have the typical architecture of this part of the island, with sloped roofs to collect precious rainwater in cisterns. No festival would be complete without a Canarian wrestling tournament, a long tradition on Lanzarote.

CATHEDRAL OF ST. MARY OF REGLA

León Cathedral, catalogued as one of the great works of the European Gothic, has the nickname of the Pulchra leonina*, the "Beauty of León".*

The cathedral was erected atop some baths built by the Legio VII Gemina, the Roman troops who founded the city of León and would remain in Hispania until the fall of the Roman Empire. In 916 King Ordoño II ordered the first cathedral to be built to thank the Lord for his victory over the Moors in the Battle of San Esteban de Gormaz, and upon his death in 924, his tomb would rest inside. Ferdinand I of León began a second, Romanesque-style cathedral, which was consecrated in 1073 during the reign of Alfonso VI. Work began on a third in 1205, this time a Gothic-style cathedral, but foundation problems would cause construction to be stopped. Work would only begin again a full half-century later in 1255, under King Alfonso X the Wise, and conclude in the 15th century. In 1631 part of the rib vault collapsed, and

Transept and stained glass windows

León Cathedral

after that problems only seemed to mount. In 1844, the state of repair of the cathedral was such that thorough renovation was required, which after several false starts finally ended in 1901, although the foundation reinforcement continued throughout the 20th century, while the stained glass windows were restored in the 21st century. All this work has provided visitors with the opportunity to admire León Cathedral in all its splendour.

The floor plan is considered to be a replica of its sister cathedral in Reims albeit slightly smaller (the central nave is 90 metres long by 30 metres high). Highlights inside include the choir's walnut stalls (15th century), the main altar that used to feature an altarpiece by the painter and miniaturist Nicolas Francés of Burgundy (today only five 15th-century panels survive), and above all, the stained glass windows, considered the world's finest after those of Chartres Cathedral. The 134 windows and 3 large rose windows were made between the 13th and 16th centuries. The stained glass of León Cathedral, like much of its other architectural features, can be traced back to the techniques used in 13th-century French stained glass making and is similar to those in the cathedrals of Reims and Amiens. The most spectacular group of windows, which portray various themes, were made between 1260 and 1300 by different workshops.

THE ROYAL PALACE

The Royal Palace is the official residence of the King of Spain, although it is only used for ceremonial purposes.

Philip V, the first Bourbon to occupy the Spanish throne, commissioned the construction of the Royal Palace to architect Felipe Juvarra; upon his death, the project was passed on to his disciple, Juan Bautista Sachetti, who had come to Spain in 1736 to erect the Royal Palace of La Granja de San Ildefonso. The Royal Palace was built atop the remains of an old Moorish fortress or *alcázar* (9th century) that had been used by the kings of Castile, particularly Henry III the Sufferer, who had converted it into his favourite residence. His son John II built the royal chapel and other premises.

The construction of the Royal Palace did not finish until 1808, which is why neither Philip V nor Ferdinand VI had the opportunity to live there. Charles III of Spain, in 1764, became the palace's first resident and commissioned Italian architect Francesco Sabatini with a significant remodelling. When the Second

West façade

Main staircase

Republic was proclaimed, the adjacent stables designed by Sabatini were demolished to make way for the impressive gardens that bear his name.

The Royal Palace, built from the granite of the Guadarrama Mountains and white Colmenar stone, contains no fewer than 3,418 rooms, among them the two-floor Royal Library furnished with mahogany bookshelves holding 4,000 manuscripts, medallions and coins. The Royal Armoury, considered to be one of the finest in the world along with the Imperial Armoury of Vienna, contains objects from the 15th century onward. The collection includes the jousting armour made for Charles I and Philip II by the best armourers in Europe, the most important perhaps the armour worn by Charles I in the Battle of Mühlberg, the same worn by the monarch in his famous portrait on horseback painted by Titian (in the Prado Museum). The Halberdier's Room, decorated with mythologically-themed frescoes painted by Tiepolo, was originally conceived as a ballroom or a banquet hall, but Charles III turned it into a room for the palace guards. The Column Room, featuring smooth pilasters and adjoining columns whose fluted shafts are crowned by the Golden Fleece, and the Gasparini Room, decorated with rococo-style Chinese stuccoes, are considered to be among the palace's most luxurious rooms and have survived to our days mostly untouched. Lastly, there is the banquet room, whose vaults were painted by Mengs, González Velázquez and Bayeu.

The Flower of Gasparini

In addition to these rooms, the imperial grand staircase is well worth a mention. Although much simpler than the one Sachetti had intended, the current staircase was designed and completed by Sabatini, who used the staircase in the Palace of Caserta as a model while fully respecting the impressive stairwell built by Sachetti. The staircase of the Royal Palace begins as a single flight until reaching the large central landing; where it divides into two parallel flights that rise in the opposite direction to the first section. The steps, made of marble from San Pablo de los Montes (Toledo), are carved from a single piece of stone, 5 metres long and with a slight rise, while the upper balustrade is decorated with lions, also made of marble.

The Throne Room

East façade and Plaza de Oriente

THE PRADO

The Prado is the most important art museum in Spain and one of the world's ten best, having a collection of over 8,000 works.

The building is the work of Juan de Villanueva, who in 1785 was commissioned by the Count of Floridablanca with the design of a grand building to house the Natural History Cabinet and the Academy of Sciences. In 1818 Maria Isabel of Portugal decided to convert it into an arts museum (opened in 1819). At that time it was called the Royal Museum of Paintings and some works from the royal collection were transferred to Madrid from the Royal Sites. Later, the museum was taken over by the government, who renamed it the National Painting and Sculpture Museum, a name it held until 1920 when it was finally given the name *Museo Nacional del Prado*. Among the Prado's most famous works are *Resurrection of Lazarus* by Juan de Flandes, Van der Weyden's *Descent from the Cross*, *The Garden of Earthly Delights* by Hieronymus Bosch, *Artemisia* by Rembrandt, *The Three Graces* by Rubens, *Las Meninas*, by Velázquez and Goya's series *The Majas*.

The Goya Gate

Las Meninas, Velázquez

REINA SOFÍA MUSEUM

The Reina Sofía Museum is home to one of the best collections of national and international modern art, among them Picasso's famous Guernica.

The museum occupies the former site of the Madrid General Hospital (18th century) a neoclassical building near Atocha railway station which was begun by José de Hermosilla and completed by Francesco Sabatini. The first hospital, St. Charles, was built in the 16th century on the wishes of Philip II, who decided to centralise into this hospital facility the various health centres that had been scattered about court. Charles III decided to reform the hospital (18th century), as it had outgrown its small facilities. In the mid-20th century, a group of artists asked the government to set up a modern art museum to display works which did not belong in the Prado. The authorities acquiesced and the Contemporary Art Museum of Spain was opened in the basement of the National Library. Its collections later went on to be exhibited in the *Ciudad Universitaria* (the University District) until 1986, when the Reina Sofía Museum was opened. In 2001, architect Jean Nouvel began work on an extension to the museum which was opened in September 2005. Jean Nouvel's design, in addition to solving the problems raised by the museum's management, established the building within Madrid's pantheon of avant-garde architectural works. The expansion meant transforming the old building's 51,297 m^2 into the 84,048 m^2 of the new one.

The Nouvel Building

***Guernica*, Picasso**

The permanent collection contains works from the greatest Spanish artists of the 20th century, such as Picasso, Salvador Dalí, Joan Miró and Juan Gris. The first of them is represented by *Guernica*, a mural painted in Paris between May and June 1937. It was commissioned to Picasso by Josep Renau, the Director General for Fine Arts in the Spanish Republic, as a way of denouncing the bombardment by fascist planes (26th April 1937) of the town of Guernica (the Basque Country). When the military dictatorship of General Franco was established in Spain, Pablo Picasso brought *Guernica* to the Museum of Modern Art in New York, where it hung until Spain finally recovered its democratic freedoms and the mural came home in 1981. First it was exhibited in the Casón del Buen Retiro, an annex to the Prado, but since 1992 it has hung in the Reina Sofía Museum.

The Surrealism movement is represented by the works of Picabia, Magritte, Domínguez and Tanguy. The museum's collection of Cubist art, in addition to works by Picasso, contains paintings by Gris, Braque, Delaunay and Léger. There is a gallery specially dedicated to the GATEPAC (*Grupo de Arquitectos y Técnicos Españoles para el Progreso de la Arquitectura Contemporánea*), a group of Spanish architects and technicians in support of the progress of contemporary architecture, which was founded in Zaragoza (October 1930) to unite those architects related to the international movements which were revolutionising cityscapes, led by Le Corbusier. The gallery contains works by Fernand Léger, such as *Peinture murale* (1924), Willi Baumeister, *Tennis Player on Yellow* (1933) and Amédée Ozenfant, *Reds Rome* (1920-1925).

THYSSEN-BORNEMISZA MUSEUM

This is one of the leading art museums in Madrid, containing a fascinating collection of old and new masters amassed by the Thyssen-Bornemisza family over more than seventy years.

The Thyssen Museum occupies historic Villahermosa Palace, renovated in 1805 in the neoclassical style by the architect Antonio López Aguado, a disciple of Juan de Villanueva. One of Madrid's noblest palaces, in 1844 it became the temporary residence of Franz Liszt, who graced its salons with several of his piano pieces.

The museum's main collection comes from the private collection of the first Baron Thyssen-Bornemisza, who started enlarging the collection of his father, August Thyssen, in 1928. The collection added some of its best works between 1928 and 1938 with paintings by Dürer, Holbein, Jan van Eyck, Vittore Carpaccio, Sebastiano del Piombo, Caravaggio, Tiepolo and Frans Hals. The museum contains over 600 works, among them the 240 from the private collection of Carmen Cervera, Baron Thyssen's widow.

The Museum Hall

Main façade

SOROLLA MUSEUM

Joaquín Sorolla, the "painter of light", defined either as an Impressionist or a Luminist, lived in Madrid, where his house and studio have become the most important museum dedicated to the artist.

Sorolla's wife, Clotilde García, gave his house and studio to the government upon his death, so a museum could be founded in her husband's honour. On 28th March 1931, the government accepted the legacy, and a year later, the Sorolla Museum opened to the public under the curatorship of Joaquín Sorolla García, the couple's only son, who occupied the post until his death in 1948.

After becoming a national museum, new canvases were acquired and today the collection has numerous pieces, among them *Walk on the Beach*, *The Horse's Bath*, *The Pink Robe*, *White Slave Trade* and *A Research*, along with sculptures by Rodin, Pedro de Mena and Mariano Benlliure, and ceramics by Zuloaga.

The Garden of the Sorolla Museum

Walk on the Beach, Sorolla

PLAZA MAYOR

The hustle and bustle of Madrid's main square has made it the place to meet for locals and foreigners alike.

The origins of the square date back to the 16th century, when the space was occupied by a market that was highly popular among the locals. The market's success soon led to the construction of the first house with arcades, an exchange to organise trading. In 1580 Philip II commissioned Juan de Herrera to thoroughly remodel the square, which led to some houses being demolished and the construction of new buildings,

The Panadería

Painter in the arcades of Plaza Mayor

such as the *Casa de la Panadería* (the Bakery House), begun in 1590 by Diego Sillero on the spot where the exchange had stood. The *Panadería*, used to stockpile bread and flour, was completed in 1612. The ground floor was occupied by the municipal bakery, while the first floor balconies and rooms were set aside for the king and queen so they could observe festivals held in the square, particularly bullfights. In 1670, after the second fire in the square, Tomás Román was commissioned to rebuild the *Panadería*, while painters Claudio Coello and José Jiménez Donoso carried out the interior decoration and the frescoes on the façade. From the mid- to late-18th century, the Panadería was home to the St. Ferdinand Royal Academy of Fine Arts, and between 1774 and 1841, the Royal Academy of History. It would later become the Municipal Library and Archive. The façade stands out for the shield with the royal coat of arms

The Panadería and the statue of Philip III

of Charles II: those of Castile and León (in the first quadrant), Aragon and Sicily (the second), Austria and modern Burgundy (the third), ancient Burgundy and Brabant (the fourth), in the centre the symbol of Granada, and in the inescutcheon, the coats of arms of Flanders and Tyrol. Opposite the *Panadería* is the *Casa de la Carnicería* (the Butcher's House), the second most important building in the square. The exact date of its construction is unknown, although it is believed to have been built after the square's first fire (1631). At the end of the 19th century, the *Carnicería* was converted into the deputy mayor's offices and the almshouse for the Audiencia district. It is currently abandoned although there is a scheme to turn it into a luxury hotel. In 1617 Philip III planned for new buildings on the Plaza Mayor which would be carried out by Juan Gómez de Mora.

Its most famous entrance, the *Arco de Cuchilleros* (the Cutlers' Arch), leads to the street of the same name which was full of cutlery workshops which supplied and sharpened the knives used by the butchers inside the square. Overlooking Plaza Mayor is a statue of Philip III on horseback, which the sculptor Giambologna and his disciple Pietro Tacca made for the Grand Duke of Florence; it used to be elsewhere before it was moved here upon the orders of Queen Isabella II, as is stated on its pedestal.

CIBELES SQUARE

Madrid's Cibeles Square, containing a fountain bearing the same name, is one of its symbols and the focal point for Real Madrid football club celebrations.

Charles III undertook a series of city planning reforms to raise Madrid to the level of grandeur of other great European capitals. With this idea in mind, he commissioned Ventura Rodríguez (18th century) with the design of an ornamental fountain, which led to the creation of the popular Cibeles fountain. The goddess Cybele and her chariot were sculpted from the marble of the Montesclaros quarries (Toledo) by Francisco Gutiérrez Arribas, while the Frenchman Robert Michel carved the lions and Miguel Jiménez the border.

At the end of the 18th century, Juan de Villanueva, the primary figure in Spanish neoclassical architecture, suggested enlarging the fountain with the sculptures of a dragon and a bear carved by Alfonso Bergaz. The water flowing from the dragon's mouth was intended for the public, while the bear used to fill the jars of water carriers; both statues were removed in 1862. Before its current location, Cibeles fountain stood in a boulevard of the Salón del Prado.

Cibeles Square

Cibeles Fountain

RETIRO PARK

The 118-hectare park is presided by a reflecting pool and a monument to Alfonso XII.

The grand expanse occupied by Retiro Park was once home to a palace, built on the orders of Philip IV, as well as nine chapels, a *corral de comedias* (a theatre courtyard) and a bull ring. The gardens were designed by Cosme Loti, the Grand Duke of Tuscany's personal designer, and used to contain wild animal cages and an exotic bird house. Charles III opened the park to the public on the condition that its visitors came "properly washed and dressed". Throughout its history the park has undergone several interventions that have changed the layout of its gardens. Charles III, for example, ordered the building of the Buen Retiro Royal Porcelain Works, popularly known as *La China*, while Charles IV had Juan de Villanueva erect an astronomical observatory.

During the Peninsular War (1808) the gardens were severely damaged by French troops, who felled various trees. Afterwards, Ferdinand VII, the "Felon King",

The reflecting pool and monument to Alfonso XII

The Crystal Palace

The statue of the *Fallen Angel*, Ricardo Bellver

began the reconstruction of the park as we know it today. Its main points of interest include the Statue Walk, flanked by the statues of various kings of Spain; the Gate of Spain, whose ironwork was designed by Agustín Felipe Peró (1893); the Crystal Palace, built in 1887 for the Exhibition of the Philippines; the Fountain of the *Fallen Angel* by the Madrid sculptor Ricardo Bellver (1885), which occupies the site of the Buen Retiro Royal Porcelain Works; the Rose Garden, planted in 1915 by Cecilio Rodríguez, head gardener of El Retiro; and the monument to Ramón y Cajal by Victorio Macho.

GRAN VÍA AVENUE

Lined with shops, theatres, cinemas, nightclubs, hotels, bars and restaurants, this is one of Spain's most famous avenues.

Gran Vía, which runs from Alcalá Street to Plaza de España, is known as the "Broadway of Madrid", particularly the section between two squares, Callao and España.

In its honour, Federico Chueca would compose a zarzuela, a traditional Spanish operetta, called *La Gran Vía*, the libretto of which was written by Felipe Pérez.

Callao Cinema and the Carrión Building

The avenue itself was designed by municipal architects José López Sallaberry and Francisco Andrés Octavio Palacios in order to connect the Argüelles and Salamanca districts, relieve the traffic-bound square of Puerta del Sol, and eliminate the labyrinth of narrow and somewhat insalubrious alleyways that encumbered the flow of both vehicles and pedestrians alike. The authorities approved the project in 1904, but work was delayed due to stiff opposition from residents (310 houses had to be knocked down) and shopkeepers. In 1909, the Gran Vía project was awarded for 29 million pesetas to Martín Albert Silver, a French banker with important business interests in London, and in 1910, to great pomp and circumstance and with King Alfonso XIII looking on, the first demolitions and excavation were begun.

Of the many interesting buildings lining the Gran Vía, most built in the historicist style, it is worth mentioning the Metropolis (1911) by architects Jules and Raymond Février; the Gran Peña, a Baroque-style military club, (1917); the Oratory of the Caballero de Gracia (1916) by Juan de Villanueva; Casa Matesanz (1919), built by Antonio Palacios; the Telefónica building (1926), one of the oldest skyscrapers in Europe and the first in Spain; the Fontalba Theatre (1919); the Palacio de la Música (1926); the Palacio de la Prensa (1924); the Carrión (1931) by architect Luis Martínez Feduchi; and in the Plaza de España, the Madrid Building (1957), the tallest building in the capital until the construction of the Picasso Tower.

Alcalá Street and Gran Vía

ST. MICHAEL'S MARKET

The market retains its original iron structure, a fine example of early 20th-century industrial architecture.

It dates back to the Middle Ages, when there was once an open-air market in the same area. The old church of St. Michael of the Octoes (where Lope de Vega was baptised) was demolished in the times of Joseph Bonaparte, and the market bearing the name of the former church was built atop the same site. In 1847, Pascual Madoz, in his famous *Diccionario*, wrote that the market had 128 *cajones* or temporary traders and 88 fixed stalls. In 1913, work was begun to cover the market, which was the custom across Europe at the time, and on 13th May 1916 the current market was opened, the only iron-frame market in Madrid to survive into our times after the demolition of the Cebada and Mostenses markets.

The structure stands out for its cast-iron pillars, the system of gutters and the decorative ceramic cresting on the roof. The glass enclosure was installed much later. The market was restored in 1999, but it had to close down due to poor profits, shuttering the

Main entrance

The iron roof and market stalls.

stalls established along its nine aisles. Nevertheless, a private group decided to revive it and turn it into a high quality delicatessen; on 13th May 2009, it opened its doors once again.

Several shops, tapas bars and other stands selling select food products have set up in St. Michael's Market. Some of the vendors even offer a free taste of the items they sell. In addition, St. Michael's Market has become one of the capital's gastronomy venues and its management has organised several entertainment and cultural events.

THE PICASSO MUSEUM

Pablo Picasso, the internationally renowned painter born in Malaga, has a museum in his native city devoted to some of his life's work.

The idea for the museum arose out of conversations between Pablo Picasso and Juan Temboury, the Provincial Delegate for Fine Art in Malaga. However, authorities in the Franco regime scuttled the project as they considered Picasso to be a political enemy, particularly after he had painted *Guernica*, a mural which internationally denounced the bombardment of civilians by Fascist aviation forces during the Spanish Civil War. Despite this, in the passage of time his importance as an artist would lead to a certain normalisation of

Buenavista Palace

Marble column and Mudéjar coffered ceiling

relations between the painter and the regime, on the condition that Picasso did not publicly express his opposition to the dictatorship. In 1992 Christine Ruiz-Picasso, the painter's daughter-in-law, revived the idea of creating a museum in her father-in-law's native city, which resulted in its opening in 2003.

The site chosen for the museum was the Palace of the Counts of Buenavista (16th century), built by the city's mayor Diego de Cazalla. The location and tower of this Renaissance-style palace has made it one of the most emblematic private buildings in Malaga. The two-storey palace, which opens into an arcaded courtyard, underwent several renovations before becoming the Picasso Museum. Architects Richard Gluckman, Rafael Martín and Isabel Delgado were commissioned to adapt the building to its new function. Two adjacent houses behind the palace ac-

Gallery in the Picasso Museum

quired for the expansion were demolished to build the temporary gallery and the events hall. The main entrance was kept in the same location, although the position of the staircase was slightly altered to make for a larger reception area. To control the light entering the interior, the skylights were fitted with double-paned glass and a system of awnings.

The museum's collection of Picasso paintings covers from his most revolutionary work to the wide variety of styles and techniques he perfected through his career. From his first academic studies to his personal vision of classicism, from his superimposed planes of Cubism to his forays into ceramics, reinterpretations of the great masters and his last paintings in the 1970s, Picasso's body of work is on display in this museum in all its glory. The galleries provide the opportunity to think about the artist's relationship with Malaga and reflect on Picasso's role in the history of art as the creator of Cubism and the invention of images that synthesise multiple formal and conceptual perspectives. His manner of interpreting the classic themes of painting, such as portraits, still-life, landscapes or nudes reveal the creative capacity of this great artist, certainly one of a kind.

ROMAN THEATRE

The Roman Theatre of Mérida, declared a World Heritage Site, still holds performances and is widely admired for its proscenium.

Emerita Augusta (Mérida), capital of Lusitania, was the tenth largest city in the Roman Empire, and it would maintain its status until the fall of the empire.

In a reflection of the city's economic importance, the theatre was built between 16 and 15 BC thanks to the support of Marcus Vipsanius Agrippa, a Roman general and consul who led some of Octavius's military victories.

Over its two-thousand year history the theatre has been the target of various renovations, particularly during the reigns of Trajan and Constantine. The current proscenium was erected in 105 and renovated between 333 and 335, along with the road surrounding the building.

General view of the Theatre

Detail of the proscenium

Buried for ages, excavation work began in 1910; it uncovered a large part of the theatre and its columns were studied and documented. In 1964 the architect and archaeologist José Menéndez Pidal took charge of the restoration, declaring it "the prince among Emeritan monuments". The architecture of the theatre follows the guidelines set down by Vitruvius for this type of building. Taking advantage of the slope of St. Martin's Hill, its semi-circular stands (*cavea*) can accommodate 6,000 spectators distributed in three areas. The twenty-two rows of seats located at the bottom were destined to the wealthier social classes. The middle and upper tiers, each with five rows of seats, were supported by a complex system of arches and barrel vaults. Six gates, located at the top of the theatre, lead to a semi-circular corridor covered by a vault that allowed spectators to enter and exit through the gates at either end. The orchestra, a semi-circular area paved by white and blue marble slabs, is surrounded by three tiers of honour for the highest authorities of the city. However, the most spectacular area is undoubtedly the stage, as it has withstood the passage of time so well. There are two sections, each with three doors with Corinthian columns, whose marble bases and cornices are richly decorated with statues.

NATIONAL MUSEUM OF ROMAN ART

This museum, located in the ancient Emerita Augusta, houses an excellent collection of objects from Roman Spain.

In the year 25 BC, the imperial legate Publius Carisius received an order from his emperor, Octavius Augustus, to found a colony for emeritus soldiers, professional servicemen who had fought in the Cantabrian wars. Publius Carisius began construction of the Emerita Augusta Colony, today Mérida, where the legions V Alaudae and X Gemina would settle. The colony would become extremely important in the Roman Empire, evidenced by the many archaeological remains that have been discovered here, as well as the medallions and coins of Publius Carisius, Augustus and Tiberius. Mark Antony once stated that Emerita Augusta had occupied the tenth position among the most important cities of the Empire, while Marcus Ausonius, a Latin poet, situated it even higher, in ninth place. Capital of the province of Lusitania, Emerita Augusta maintained its economic might until the fall of the Western Roman Empire.

The importance of the Roman remains discovered in Mérida caused the authorities to consider building a great museum to store them and display them to the public. The project came into being on 19th September 1986 when the modern museum replaced the former Archaeological Museum of Mérida, founded in 1838. The new building was designed by architect Rafael Moneo, who formulated an architectonic language that proposed a return to the past in terms of techniques, significance and content, yet without ignoring the present.

The museum's collections can be traced back to the 16th century, with the pieces that had been stowed away in the palace of Fernando Vera y Vargas. From

Central gallery

Central gallery

these initial items, and others discovered in the many archaeological excavations made in Mérida, the first museum was created in 1838. Currently the museum's collection contains over 37,000 objects, the most noteworthy being sculptures, mosaics and coins. In addition, there is a fine selection of ceramic and glass items. The precious metalwork at the museum includes several rings carved with various depictions, a silver fibula (4th century) from the Las Tiendas villa, and several gold threads discovered in a tomb.

CATHEDRAL OF THE HOLY SAVIOUR

Oviedo Cathedral, called Sancta Ovetensis ("the Saint of Oviedo") due to the number of relics it contains, was built atop a pre-Romanesque church.

The construction of the cathedral was begun in the last quarter of the 13th century and finished in the 16th century with the completion of the bell tower (70 metres high). The ambulatory and several chapels in the side naves were added in the 17th century. The interior contains an *Apostolate* composed of the twelve disciples of Christ arranged in pairs, making for one of the most important arrangements of its kind from the Spanish Romanesque period. Its main altarpiece (16th century) is considered the third best in Spain, after the altarpieces in the cathedrals of Toledo and Seville.

The 9th-century pre-Romanesque Holy Chamber, the chief area of interest in the cathedral, has been devoted to keeping its relics and treasures since its construction, the defence of which led to the erection of the Old Tower. The two chapels forming the Holy Chamber,

Central nave and main altar

The Cathedral Square

Cross of the Angels (9th century)

which are not interconnected, contain the treasures of Spanish precious metalworking, such as the Agate Box (10th century) donated by Princess Fruela of Asturias and the Victory Cross (10th century), a gift from Alfonso III the Great, as well as the Cross of the Angels, a consular diptych, the Holy Ark, the little box of Bishop Ariano, etc. The most important piece, the Cross of the Angels (9th century), was made for Alfonso II of Asturias, according to the inscription it bears. This Greek-style cross is made of gold-plated wood encrusted with precious stones and pearls.

FONTÁN MARKET

Fontán Square, a typical place in the capital of Asturias to have some culines*, a few glasses of local Asturian cider, is next to a market as colourful as it is popular amongst the locals.*

Fontán Market, Oviedo's most important, was first documented in Council of Oviedo ordinances back in the 13th century. The market is still very much alive and its stalls have an air of country life.

During Christmas of 1521, a devastating fire broke out which ravaged part of the city of Oviedo. Two years later, in 1523, Charles I of Spain, in an attempt to help the population overcome the economic crisis brought on by the fire, granted the citizens of Oviedo the privilege of holding a tax-exempt market every Thursday, starting in 1524. The spot chosen for the market was the Fontán, an area that was once a lake that had been drained a few years before to prevent the spread of illnesses. The last vestiges of the waters

Market stalls

The arcades of Fontán Market

that still flowed here are represented by the Caño del Fontán, a fountain that decorates the square.

The construction of the current market, designed by architect Javier Aguirre, was begun in 1882 and completed in 1885. The building, protected by the local government as a city monument, has the typical industrial architecture so in vogue in the 19th century for these types of establishments. The market is the city's premier place for perishable food shopping, as it has the highest concentration of speciality food establishments. Its stalls are packed with cold meats, sausages and cheese from all over Spain, but in particular the famous cheeses of Asturias, such as *Cabrales*, not to mention legumes, fresh fish, cider, fruit and vegetables, salted meat and fish, pickled goods and an endless list of products related to traditional Asturian cookery.

The 2,000-m^2 market, in addition to supplying a great variety of foodstuffs, has become quite a tourist attraction, as there are countless restaurants located in the vicinity to sample the regional cooking.

PRE-ROMANESQUE ASTURIAN ART

Pre-Romanesque Asturian art, developed between the 8th and the early 10th century, mostly in Asturias but also in the neighbouring area of Cantabria, has specific characteristics owing to the fact the region remained outside the control of Moorish Spain. Although pre-Romanesque Asturian art succeeded Visigothic art, experts insist that it cannot be considered a direct heir as it displayed its own particular characteristics.

After Ramiro I of Asturias took the throne (reigning from 842 to 850), Asturian art reached its zenith, even though the monarch would only rule for eight years. During this period the signature works of

Church of St. Christine of Lena

Church of St. Michael of Lillo

Asturian art found on Mount Naranco, classified as the Ramirian style due to its sponsorship by the king, adopted Greek-cross floor plans, square apses, barrel vaults and transverse arches.

Experts suggest that buildings from the time of Ramiro I were in fact the work of the same architect, due to their great similarity to one another and peculiar common features: the vaulted ceilings, a tribune above the portico, the arches nearly always fitted with stone voussoirs, the Eastern motif decoration, the introduction of human and animal figures, and the depiction of the Greek cross with the alpha and omega. The work considered the masterpiece

Church of St. Mary at Mount Naranco

of Asturian art is **St. Mary at Mount Naranco**, a former palace belonging to Ramiro I that was converted into a church. The ground floor takes the form of a covered room whose windowless vaults have three well-defined sections: the central one for the guards and servants, another for the chapel and a third containing a tank. The upper storey is a rectangular room with a barrel vault and transverse arches, which opens at the ends in a triple arch. The decoration of the arches and mouldings imitates precious metalwork and marquetry. The other great work of the Ramirian period is **St. Michael of Lillo**, the only church to use columns and not pillars, and it was used as a palace temple by Ramiro I, as shown by its sculptural decoration. Lastly, **St. Christine of Lena**, originally a Visigoth temple that was renovated by Ramiro I, contains a triple-arched iconostasis.

ST. MARY'S CATHEDRAL

Majorca Cathedral, with its pinnacles and flying buttresses, overlooks the Mediterranean Sea.

St. Mary's Cathedral, called *La Seu* in Majorcan (the See), was built atop the former Grand Mosque of Palma, which was consecrated as a Christian temple after James I of Aragon conquered the island. Shortly after the King ordered the building of the cathedral, the mosque was demolished. James II of Majorca wrote in his testament that it was his desire to be buried at the cathedral, and to comply with his wishes the Trinity Chapel was built, whose style can be traced to the work of Poncio Descoyl. Since 1947 the Trinity Chapel has safeguarded the tombs of James II (1243-1311) and James III (1315-1349) in beautiful sarcophagi supported upon lions sculpted by Frederic Marès.

Majorca Cathedral is an amalgam of different styles as its construction took over three centuries to complete. The 14th-century Mirador Portal, the most ornate, contains a sculpted mullion and tympanum, two archivolts with figures and five statues. The finest parts of the Cathedral are its rose windows, among the best preserved in Spain from the Gothic period.

Majorca Cathedral

Majorca Cathedral and walls

THE ROYAL PALACE OF LA ALMUDAINA

La Almudaina – the Citadel – sits high above Palma de Mallorca and was built by Arabs upon the remains of a Roman fort.

James I of Aragon, after conquering the island of Majorca, established his residence in the former Moorish citadel. His son James II undertook (1309) the transformation from fortress to royal palace based on the plans of the Majorcan Pedro Salvá, the builder of Bellver Castle. The new palace served as the court of the monarchs of the Kingdoms of Majorca and Aragon, and is currently the official residence of the King and Queen of Spain.

Main Room

The only reminder the Palace of the Almudaina retains of its Moorish past is its name; the rest was erased by the Christian kings after conquering the island. The Palace's current design corresponds to the 14th century. The north façade, in the northwest corner, contains a reproduction of the tower at Perpignan Castle. The most important, however, is the south façade, which retains its twin towers, the semi-circular arcades of its ground-floor portico, a gallery of pointed arches above, and on the top level a series of ogive windows. Above it all rises the Angel of La Almudaina, the guardian angel of Majorca, a 14th-century sculpture by Antonio de Camprodón, carved in Perpignan for King James II of Aragon. The angel wears a tunic and holds a cross in her left hand, while the shield upon her breast bears the inscription *Et verbum caro factum est* ("And the Word became flesh"). The angel, also a weather vane, points in the direction where the wind is blowing with her right arm and forefinger. The festival honouring this angel, celebrated on the day after Easter Sunday, was one of the four most important festivals held on the island of Majorca during the Middle Ages.

Inside the building, in the King's Courtyard, is the Chapel of St. Anne; in another courtyard – similarly

La Almudaina and the walls from the Park del Mar

The Guardian Angel of La Almudaina

named the Queen's – is the tower keep, which rises from the lower part of the building. The ground floor is recreated in the medieval style with artwork from the 15th to the 20th centuries, while the upper level, used by the Spanish royal family for official events, is decorated with furniture of the *Patrimonio Nacional* (the National Heritage) from the 17th to 19th centuries. The chief highlight is the Gothic royal chapel with its square apse, royal tribune on the evangelist side bearing the coats of arms of the Catholic Monarchs, and the rib vault whose intersections are adorned with circular paintings devoted to the Annunciation, the Good Shepherd and the Coronation of the Virgin.

THE UNIVERSITY

The University of Salamanca, the oldest in Spain still holding classes, obtained its title thanks to a Papal bull from Pope Alexander IV.

Founded in 1218, the former General School, which gave classes in canonical and civil law, medicine, logic, grammar and music, was converted into a university in 1255 under Alfonso X after the corresponding papal authorisation. At first, the professors taught their students in the cloister of the old cathedral, some houses rented from the city hall and St. Benedict's Church. The construction of the university began in the 15th century and lasted until the 16th. Various renovations and expansion took place in the centuries to come. In the 17th century, for example, the library was demolished to make way for the current one in the 18th century.

The frog and skull

The historical importance of the University of Salamanca is such that its cloister was the site where Christopher Columbus argued for the viability of his plan. And after his discovery of America, the need to recognise the rights of the natives was put forth in the very same cloister. It was mathematicians from the University of Salamanca who analysed the reformation of the calendar thought up by Pope Gregory XIII and proposed a solution that was later implemented. Among its many professors, it is worth mentioning Friar Luis de León.

The architectural features of the University come from Renaissance civil building, and it is arranged over a square floor plan, a central courtyard, surrounding galleries and a cloister staircase. The main façade is divided into three sections and is considered one of the best examples of the Spanish Plateresque. Built in 1411, the first section displays a medallion of the Catholic Monarchs, who are portrayed holding a sceptre, while the yoke of Ferdinand and the arrows of Isabella sit above their heads. The second section

Cloister

contains the coat of arms of Charles I of Spain, complete with a globe and cross; to his right he gazes upon an eagle, the symbol of John the Evangelist, and to his left is the two-headed eagle of the Empire. The third section has a small chapel dedicated to Pope Benedict XIII, the *Papa Luna*, and to Pope Martin V. The portal was dedicated to the Catholic Monarchs in 1534. Curiously, there is a sculpture of a frog on the portal as well, which over time has become an icon of the city. The frog is sitting atop the parietal of a human skull. The intentions of the sculptor who carved the frog remain a puzzle to historians, who have put forth any number of reasons to explain its significance. Some experts see the frog and skull as an allegory for death, as it was in Ancient Egypt.

PLAZA MAYOR

The centre of Salamanca's social life, Miguel de Unamuno, who took part in many a discussion at the Café Novelty, described it as an irregular yet delightfully harmonious rectangle.

The Plaza Mayor of Salamanca, built between 1729 and 1755 in the Baroque style, was initially planned by Alberto Churriguera and later completed by other architects. Its design is similar to that of main squares in other Spanish cities, such as the Plaza Mayor in Madrid, the Plaza Ochavado in Valladolid and the Plaza Cuadrado in Cordoba. However, the structure is largely devoid of any fine materials, such as marble or alabaster, and it was only in 1752 that the 6 marble shields of the city were installed.

Various renovations were made in the early 19th century, while in the 20th century its gardens, bandstand and public lavatories were removed. Its origins can be traced back to a plot next to the city walls used by vendors to sell their wares. Overlooking the area was the former St. Martin's Church, which is where the former square got its name. In 1935 the square received the title of National Monument for being one of the most decorated of its epoch. Traffic through the square was banned in the 1970s, and it

Plaza Mayor

Salamanca City Hall in Plaza Mayor

soon recovered its spirit as a popular gathering place. The square was built in two phases; first, two pavilions were built, the Royal and St. Martin's Pavilions, while the second phase consisted of building the city hall and its façade (1750-1756), a task commissioned to architect Juan García Berruguilla. The perimeter of the square was enclosed on 29th April 1755.

The square is upheld by 88 rounded arches, whose semi-circular shape was heavily used in Romanesque architecture, while the spandrels (the triangular-shaped spaces in an arch) feature carved medallions depicting figures related to the history of the city. There are coats of arms emblazoned on the main arches, balconies and other elements. On the main arch, near the market exit, there is an inscription bearing testament to a gruesome event: "Here a woman was killed, pray to God for her. 1838".

In the 1950s, boys would go round the square in one direction and girls in another so they could catch a glimpse of each other every time they went round. Today the Plaza Mayor of Salamanca has become a gathering place for visitors and locals alike to frequent its many bars and restaurants.

ST. JAMES'S CATHEDRAL

The city of Santiago de Compostela grew around the tomb of the apostle who gave the town its name, which drew thousands of pilgrims during the Middle Ages and became the centre of European spirituality.

Rising above Obradoiro Square is St. James's Cathedral, and according to widespread tradition, it contains the tomb of the apostle of the same name. Declared a World Heritage Site by UNESCO in 1985, the cathedral started to grow during the reign of Alfonso III, who built a pre-Romanesque church, consacrated in 889, in order to accommodate the great number of pilgrims coming to visit the tomb.

The current cathedral has a monumental Baroque façade overlooking Obradoiro Square, designed by Casas de Novoa (1740). However, the most remarkable part of the entire cathedral is the Romanesque-style Portico of Glory, which was constructed between 1168 and 1188 to a design by the master builder Mateo on a commission from King Ferdinand II, who paid the annual sum of one hundred thousand maravedis to build it. Divided into three rounded arches, the centre one consists of a mullion with a sculpture of St. James.

St. James the Apostle in the Mullion on the Portico of Glory

Obradoiro façade

THE AQUEDUCT

The presence of Rome can be felt across Segovia, but nowhere more so than by its aqueduct, which stands in its own right as one of the greatest Roman constructions in Europe.

The precise date of the Aqueduct (from the Latin *aqua* for "water" and *ducere* for "drive") of Segovia is not precisely known, but several authors point to the end of the 1st or 2nd centuries. The 794-metre long aqueduct (16.2 kilometres including the entire length of the channel) was built using 20,400 unmortared granite blocks and transported water to the city from the Fuenfría Spring (the aqueduct was in use until the 19th century). In Roman times, there was a bronze plaque (since disappeared) posted on the three tallest arches which bore the date of its construction and the name of the master builder. One of the niches, which can still be seen today, used to have a statue of Hercules who, according to legend, founded the city of Segovia. Currently two of the niches display images of the Virgin Mary of Fuencisla, the patron saint of Segovia, and St. Stephen.

Two thousand years of history have left many a mark upon the stones of the Aqueduct of Segovia, not to mention plenty of damage, particularly from the various houses that adjoined the structure until 1860 and hindered passage beneath the arches. Little by little, the National Heritage authorities became aware of the importance of preserving the aqueduct, and after a meticulous restoration, it has all the splendour of the finest days of the Roman epoch. To preserve it, traffic was banned from travelling beneath its structure, although this did not appear to affect the stability of the aqueduct due to the great inertia of its mass.

Night view of the Aqueduct

View from the walls

ALCÁZAR

Two monuments of Segovia attract everyone's attention: the Aqueduct and the Alcázar, whose oldest stone blocks are quite similar to those used to build the aqueduct.

The origins of the Alcázar might date back to an ancient Roman fortress. The Arabs built a fortress on this spot as well, which the Christian kings later enlarged and refurbished until Philip II decided upon the form seen today. In the Middle Ages, the Alcázar was used as the residence of the kings of Castile, mainly by Alfonso X the Wise. The Alcázar was considered among the most luxurious royal palaces of the 15th century, but a fire in 1862 would destroy its ornate ceilings which had to be rebuilt according to the original plans.

The main feature of the Alcázar is its great square-shaped tower keep, which has four keeps with barrel vault roofs and mullioned windows. The inside is richly decorated, such as the Throne Room, which has an octagonal truss ceiling (15th century). The walls bear the portraits of the Catholic Monarchs.

South façade and the Tower of John II

View of the Alcázar

CATHEDRAL AND THE GIRALDA

The Cathedral of St. Mary of the See, the largest Gothic cathedral in the world, was built upon the site of the mosque of Seville.

Seville Cathedral was built on the site of the former Almohad mosque, which in turn was constructed atop the old Roman forum in the 9th century by Abd ar-Rahman II (who died in Cordoba in 852). The 1977 excavations proved that before the mosque there had been an old Visigoth basilica from the 5th century and its corresponding baptistery, which is believed to be the site of St. Vincent's Church where St. Isidore of Seville was buried.

After the conquest of Seville by Ferdinand III the Saint (1248), the city was Christianised, leading to the fervent construction of churches, convents and chapels. According to tradition, work on the cathedral began in 1401, although the oldest known plans date from 1490.

Seville Cathedral

The five naves inside are an amalgam of different styles (Mudéjar, Plateresque, Gothic, and so on) due to its lengthy period of construction. The 16th-century Royal Chapel, the work of the master builders Pedro Ruiz de Palacios and Juan de Maeda, is well worth admiring for its decoration, particularly the main altarpiece by the sculptor Ruiz Ortiz de Vargas, who worked on it between 1643 and 1649, carving the images of St. Joachim and St. Anne in polychrome wood. The centre panel has an image of the Virgin Mary of the Kings, which Alfonso X had brought from his palace to the church. Note the hair of the Virgin Mary made from gold and silk thread. The silver altar frontal (18th century) is the work of Villaviciosa, the famed silversmith. The altar also contains an interesting ivory carving of the Virgin Mary of Battles, called as such because, according to tradition, it would always accompany Ferdinand III onto the battlefield. Another area of the cathedral well worth mentioning is the main sacristy (16th century) with a Plateresque entranceway.

Outside Seville's cathedral stands perhaps its most outstanding feature, the Giralda (104 m tall, including the Giraldillo), a bell tower whose lower two thirds were part of the minaret of the Almohad mosque. Rising above the bell room, built by Hernán Ruiz in 1558, is a tower crowned by the Giraldillo, a wind vane considered one of the largest bronze sculptures of the Renaissance. Tradition says that the construction of the minaret is owed to the famous alchemist Geber, but it was several *alarifes* (Moorish master builders) who were actually in charge of building it, among them Alí de Gomara who changed the granite blocks for fired bricks to cut costs.

The Giralda

ROYAL ALCÁZAR

Ancient Hispalis for the Romans, the "city on the Guadalquivir River" still preserves its Royal Alcázar, a palatial fortification considered the oldest royal palace in Europe.

The first palace of the current Alcázar was built in 712 after the city was conquered by Moorish troops, and it is known to have been occupied by the city's first sheikhs in 720. The original structure can still be seen in the Almohad walls and the Patio del Yeso (Plasterwork Courtyard). After Ferdinand III the Saint reconquered Seville, the king and his successors would take up residence in the palace. Alfonso X the Wise began its first major renovation, ordering the construction of three large rooms in 1254. In 1364 King Peter I of Castile built the richly-decorated Mudéjar Palace, which would later be refurbished by the Catholic Monarchs and the first Austrian kings. In their wanders through the halls of the Royal Alcázar, visitors will come across ornately tiled rooms and the delicate ornamentation of Mudéjar ceilings. The main courtyard, or the Court of the Maidens,

Detail of the tile decoration in the Court of the Maidens

is considered a masterpiece of Mudéjar-Andalusian artwork. Next to it are the royal quarters and opposite is the Ambassador's Room, whose door is decorated with peacocks. To its left is the Charles I of Spain Room, whose coffered ceilings contain the royal coat of arms. The rooms still have several Flemish tapestries (18th century) to match the tile skirting boards by Cristóbal de Augusta (16th century).

Among the numerous ceramic objects preserved in the Royal Alcázar, the highlight perhaps is the tiled altar (16th century) made by Francisco Niculoso Pisano for the oratory of the Catholic Monarchs.

The Royal Alcázar Gardens remind visitors of the famous figures who once strolled through them, such

Detail of the stuccoes in the Prince's bedroom

The Ambassadors Room

as Maria de Padilla, famous for her love affair with King Peter I of Castile, or Isabella I of Castile, the Catholic Queen. The gardens are decorated by several tile, cut marble and bronze fountains.

Court of the Maidens

MARIA LUISA PARK

The park, an authentic breath of fresh air in Seville, is located in the rectangle formed by Isabel la Católica Avenue and Paseo de las Delicias, a boulevard running parallel to the Guadalquivir River.

Infanta Maria Luisa Fernanda de Borbón (1832-1897), Ferdinand VII's daughter and the Duchess of Montpensier through her marriage to Antoine of Orleans, the Duke of Montpensier, decided to donate half the gardens of her St. Elmo Palace to the city of Seville in 1893. The land lacked any sense of organisation, while the plants had completely overgrown due to a lack of care. In 1911 the city of Seville commissioned a French landscape architect, Jean Claude Nicolas Forestier, to arrange the terrain, and he turned its original Renaissance design into a French-style garden full of Parisian flair.

The enormous Maria Luisa Park (340,000 m^2) made for the perfect site of the Ibero-American Exposition of 1929, although most of the work was done between 1912 and 1922. In any case, the park was officially opened under its current name on 18th April 1914. After the Exposition concluded, and in the aftermath of the New York Stock Market Crash, the gardens were abandoned and would not reopen until 1956.

On 12th July 1983, Maria Luisa Park received the distinction of Cultural Heritage Site as a Historic Garden, and today it is one of Spain's most beautiful city parks.

Its broad paths and promenades are home to numerous plant species, making for a true botanical garden, not to mention various species of birds, dozens of decorative fountains and gazebos. The Plaza de América, designed between 1911 and

The Gardens and Reflecting Pool

Plaza de América and the Mudéjar Pavilion

Bécquer Gazebo

1919, contains three former Exposition pavilions: the Mudéjar or Ancient Art Pavilion, today the Museum of Traditional Arts and Customs, the Royal Pavilion, and the Fine Arts Pavilion, which is today the Archaeological Museum; all three were built by architect Aníbal González of Seville. Another inheritance left over from the Ibero-American Exposition is the Domecq Pavilion, built by Aurelio Gómez Millán so fairgoers could sample the products of the famous Domecq Wineries. For many years after the Exposition, the pavilion was used as the headquarters of the Provincial Weather Service, and today it is home to Seville's classical music association, Juventudes Musicales.

MOUNT TEIDE PARK

Mount Teide, which occupies the centre of the park that bears its name, was formed by the eruptions of the volcano whose crater is covered in snow for much of the year.

Teide National Park was created in 1954, although the first attempts to protect its *cañadas* (the flat terrain between the mountain ridges) date back to the era of the Second Republic. In 1934, the chief engineer of the forest district of Santa Cruz de Tenerife, Leoncio Oramas, requested that the director of the National Forestry Administration declare the *cañadas* of Mount Teide a national park. The reasons he gave place special emphasis on the mountain's scientific interest, tourist value and cultural importance.

The geological formation of the park can be explained by three theories: an explosive crater, a collapsed caldera and an erosion caldera. The geologist Hausen considered the area to be created according to the second theory (a collapsed caldera) and noted that the mountains forming a circle around Las Cañadas are the remains of a gigantic cone atop an original basalt rock foundation. The height was much higher than the current Mount Teide and was formed over three stages. First, there was the collapsed caldera,

The Cañadas

Cinchado Rock with Mount Teide in the distance

then a period of erosion, and lastly a great deal of volcanic activity. Mount Teide itself, the highest point in Spain (3,718 m), rises from inside the Cañadas, a great helical caldera 16 kilometres wide. The park is thus formed by the great caldera of the Cañadas and the Teide-Chamorra massif rising from its interior. The native flora and fauna are truly fascinating. The chief vertebrate species is the Western Canary lizard *(Gallotia galloti)*, native to the islands of Tenerife and La Palma, and the only reptile found in the park. To fully comprehend the importance of its flora, studied for the first time by Alexander von Humboldt, one needs look no further than the 200 native species threatened by extinction compiled by the official guide to Canary plants, (*Libro rojo de la flora canaria*, 1994), which included the bencomia *(Bencomia extipulata)*, a plant growing at the park's highest peaks where only a few specimens survive.

Although Tenerife is an island with a pleasant climate, even known as the "island of Eternal Spring", Mount Teide is often covered in snow for part of the year (from mid-autumn until spring), making for a perfect picture.

MUDÉJAR TOWERS

The Mudéjar, an ornamental architectural style that flourished in Castile, Aragon and Andalusia, reached its maximum splendour in the capital of Teruel province.

Mudéjar art, which flourished between the 13th and 15th centuries, left an important mark on the artistic heritage of Teruel, especially on the towers of St. Mary's Cathedral and the churches of St. Peter, St. Martin and the Holy Saviour. Thanks to the great value of their Mudéjar art, these monuments were declared World Heritage Sites by UNESCO.

The Cathedral of Teruel was originally St. Mary's Church, a Romanesque church (12th century) which was completed when its Mudéjar tower was built in 1257. Square in shape, it is divided into three sections decorated with tiles and ceramic glazing and an octagonal cupola. The bottom of the tower has a cannon vault arch beneath it to allow for foot and vehicle traffic. The bell tower of St. Peter's Church (13th century) is considered the oldest example of the Aragonese Mudéjar style. The interior of the church was decorated in 1896 in a neo-Mudéjar style and one of its chapels contains the mortal remains of the famous "lovers of Teruel". St. Martin's Tower was erected in the 14th century and refurbished in the 16th century. Lastly, the Holy Saviour's Tower, inside the former walled city and a few steps from the Guadalaviar Gate, has a pointed arch at its base and has a decoration similar to that found in St. Martin's

Cathedral tower

Tower. The tower's decoration, according to experts, is even more perfectly executed, as can be seen in the increasingly larger sections of ornamental brick wall. As for the ceramics, copper oxide was used for the green tiles, and tin plate for the white ones, followed by lead in the glazing.

St. Peter's Tower

St. Ma-tin's Tower

ST. MARY'S CATHEDRAL

The cathedral of Toledo was given the nickname of "la Giganta" by the famous writer Blasco Ibáñez, meaning "the Giant".

Legend says that the cathedral was constructed atop a Visigoth church built around the pillar where the Virgin Mary would vest St. Ildefonsus in a chasuble. The saint had vehemently defended Mary's virginity, so to thank him for his devotion, one day the Virgin descended from the heavens to vest him in the chasuble while was preparing to say mass. This miracle, depicted by one of Berceo's works, would be repeated over the centuries again and again until it became a symbol of the city of Toledo.

The cathedral, built on the site of a former mosque and atop a Visigoth temple, began to take shape in 1226 when Ferdinand III the Saint laid its first stone. Four years earlier, in 1222, Pope Honorius III had given his blessing to build the cathedral of Toledo. The work lasted nearly three centuries and was finally completed in 1493 in the period of the Catholic Monarchs with the enclosure of the vault at the base of the central nave. The cathedral's size is spectacular: at 120 metres long and 60 wide it is one of the largest in the Christian world.

The Portal of the Clock

Toledo Cathedral

The Gothic-style exterior stands out for the Mudéjar vestiges of its bell tower (15th century), built according to the design of Flemish sculptor and architect Hanequin of Brussels, as well as the Portal of the Lions, also known as the Portal of Joy or *Puerta Nueva* (the New Portal). Built in 1460, it too is a work by Hanequín of Brussels, this time in collaboration with Pedro and Juan Guas and Juan Alemán. The image of the Assumption and other smaller sculptures were added to the portal's statuary in the 18th century. The highlights of the cathedral's interior include the main chapel with its 16th-century Gothic altarpiece by Copín of Holland and Felipe Bigarny, as well as the *Transparente* altar (18th century), an altar behind the main chapel which is illuminated from above by a Baroque skylight that lets sunshine fall directly onto the tabernacle.

ST. MARY THE WHITE

The great legacy of Toledo, the city of the three cultures (Christian, Muslim and Jewish), contains one of the jewels of Hebrew art, the synagogue of St. Mary the White.

This 12th century synagogue, founded by Jews after being granted a special permit by King Alfonso VIII, held temple prayers for more than two centuries. In 1391, after an assault on the city's Jewish quarters, the synagogue fell into Christian hands and was consecrated as the Church of St. Mary the White under the jurisdiction of the Order of Calatrava. Later on in 1550, Cardinal Siliceo transformed it into a community for repentant prostitutes. The construction was commissioned to Antonio de Covarrubias and its altarpiece by Juan Bautista Vázquez and Nicolás Vergara dates from that period. During the Peninsular War (19th century) it was somewhat damaged, as it had been reconverted into an armoury. Lastly, in 1930 the government declared it a National Monument. After the Civil War of 1936-1939, it once again returned to the Church and reconstruction was begun.

The synagogue, built in 1180 (the year 4940 in the Hebrew calendar) according to an inscription found on one of its beams, had five naves separated by pillars upholding horseshoe arches. In the Mudéjar style and constructed by Arab master builders, the walls stand out for their immaculate whiteness, the geometrical decoration of the friezes and the plant motifs on the pillar capitals. The exterior, however, is markedly austere. The layout of the naves and other characteristics recall the type of building often found in mosques of the Maghreb. The brick columns, finished in a coat of cement and lime and decorated with pinecones and scrolls, are crowned by Romanesque-style capitals. There is remarkable abstract

Tile work at the entrance

Horseshoe arches

Decoration of the pillars

ornamentation above the horseshoe arches, whose horizontal friezes and mouldings have delicate motifs based on the interaction of lines and medallions. Studies have identified the synagogue of St. Mary the White with the former "New" synagogue, which was financed by Josef ben Shoshan, prince of the Castilian Jews and treasurer of Alfonso VIII. Around 1250 a fire broke out in the synagogue, which took ten years to rebuild.

EL GRECO MUSEUM

This museum contains some of the most important works of El Greco, a Mannerist painter and native of Crete, who produced most of his oeuvre in Toledo.

Doménikos Theotokópoulos, better known as El Greco ("The Greek"), established himself in Toledo in 1577 after having travelled to Venice, where he forged ties with Titian and Tintoretto, and Rome, where he learned the Mannerism of Michelangelo. Some historians claim that he had come to Spain in the hopes of finding work at the Monastery of El Escorial and that before settling in Toledo, he had first spent a period in Madrid. Considered by some to be the first grand master of Spanish painting, El Greco always signed his paintings using Greek letters and developed his style on his native Crete (he was born in Heraklion), initially inspired by Byzantine paintings which employed traditional iconography, along with gold backgrounds and egg tempera painting techniques.

His museum was built over the remains of a 14th-century house that had belonged to Samuel Ha-Leví,

Museum gallery

***View and Plan of Toledo,* El Greco**

the treasurer of Peter I, and a Renaissance palace, both of which were located in the old Jewish quarter near the painter's home. The current building dates from the early 20th century, when the Marquis ofValle Inclán and Manuel Bartolomé Cossío, an El Greco scholar, bought the two buildings and commissioned various craftsmen from Toledo to rebuild them. The museum opened its doors on 12th June 1911, and since then it has been one of the most-visited sights in Toledo. Recreating a typical home of 16th-century Toledo, the museum contains some of El Greco's most famous paintings, such as an *Apostolate*, formed by twelve canvases of the Apostles presided by another of the Saviour, which once hung in the former poorhouse of St Sebastian; the painting *View and Plan of Toledo*, one of the most emblematic works in the museum displaying all the grandeur of the Imperial City; and a depiction of *St. Bernardine of Siena*, one of the last saint depictions painted by El Greco. His paintings denote a profound spirituality and certain air of mysticism, reflecting his profound religious beliefs.

Toledo and the Tagus River

EL GRECO

Doménikos Theotokópoulos (Heraklion, 1541-Toledo, 1614), known as "El Greco", spent his first twenty-six years of life on the island of Crete, at that time pertaining to the Republic of Venice, where he would gain fame as a master painter of post-Byzantine style icons. In 1566, El Greco requested the permission of the Venetian authorities to auction off a panel of the Passion, which fetched a price of 70 gold ducats, a value similar to those by Titian or Tintoretto. He then left for Italy, where he resided in Venice and Rome and learnt the techniques of Renaissance art. By 1576 he had come to Spain, answering Philip II's call for Italian artists to work on the Monastery of El Escorial, and in the spring of 1577 he settled in Toledo. It was in this city of La Mancha that he received his first commissions: the main altarpiece in the Church of Santo Domingo el Antiguo and a painting, *The Disrobing of Christ*, for the cathedral sacristy. These works would solidify his growing prestige. In fact, the fame of the painter was reaching such heights that many of his clients requested copies of his most famous paintings and El Greco had his workshop assistants do them. These replicas have resulted in quite a problem for specialists when having to authenticate El Greco's paintings.

The Burial of the Count of Orgaz

His painting is famous for its rather stylised figures whose altered proportions cannot be explained by mere coincidence: their heads are elongated, the fabric folds seem rustled by an upward wind, the groups of people tend to narrow, almost compress, their hands are lightweight and their sharp-edged fingers appear to emanate spirituality. On the other hand, the figures' lower extremities display more solidity, like they were weights dragging them down, accentuating even further the rising sensation of the rest of the body. The genius of El Greco allows the expression of his figures to perfectly adapt to their disproportions. According to experts, this way of understanding painting owes to the fact that El Greco worked in the complete absence of nature, without gravity or density.

Gentleman with his Hand
at his Breast

THE CATHEDRAL AND MICALET

The variety of styles, from the Gothic to the Neoclassical, found in this Cathedral devoted to St. Mary is a testament to the six centuries it took to build.

At the wish of King John I the Conqueror, the building of the Cathedral of Valencia was begun in the 13th century upon the site of the former great mosque, which in turn had been built atop a 5th-century Visigoth church. The project was commissioned to Arnau Vidal, who designed a church along rather simple architectural lines so it could be built quickly and cheaply, demarcating the territory of the Christians against the Saracens.

Our Lady's Square

The chief features on the exterior of the cathedral are the mostly Romanesque Portal of the Palace, the Gothic-style Portal of the Apostles containing various sculptures and an oculus in the shape of the star of David, and the Portal of the Irons with a magnificent Baroque iron gate. Inside, most visitors head straight to the chapel of the Holy Chalice or the Holy Grail where, despite a lack of official documentation, tradition insists the chalice of the Last Supper is guarded, the same holy grail searched far and wide by the medieval knights, mainly the Templars.

The Micalet, the Cathedral's bell tower, was begun in 1381 on the orders of James of Aragon, the bishop of Valencia and first cousin of King Peter IV of Aragon. Its first architect, Andreu Julià, was unable to finish it, and he was succeeded by José Franch, who took inspiration from the bell tower of the See of Lleida. He too, like his predecessor, could not finish the task, and it was finally completed by Martín Llobet (15th century). The bell gable was built at a later date, between 1660 and 1736. The octagonal-shaped Micalet (51 metres high at the terrace and 63 at its highest point) was built in the Levantine Gothic style and contains several bells. The bell gable contains the two clock bells: the one rung at the quarter hour (1736) and the hour bell (1539). At first the tower stood alone, until the cathedral elongated its central nave at the end of the 15th century.

Micalet Tower

CITY OF ARTS AND SCIENCES

The *Ciutat de les Arts i les Ciències*, whose first buildings were completed in 1998 with the opening of the *Hemisfèric*, was completed with the 2005 opening of its performing arts centre, the *Palau de les Arts Reina Sofía*. The architect Santiago Calatrava and engineers Alberto Domingo and Carlos Lázaro were put in charge of the project for this enormous entertainment and cultural space. After the "*gran riada*", the great flash flood of the Turia River in 1957, city authorities decided to divert the flow of the river away from the city, leaving several empty lots behind. In the 1980s, much of this area became the Turia Gardens. The rest of the old riverbed is today the site of the City of Arts and Sciences.

The ultra-modern design of the City has turned it into Valencia's main tourist attraction, not counting its magnificent beaches, and the site consists of various buildings designed for different uses. The *Hemisfèric*, in the form of an eye, contains a screening room and a planetarium. The Prince Felipe Science Museum displays the latest scientific advances and discoveries. The *Umbracle* contains an art gallery

The Science Museum and the *Hemisfèric*

Reina Sofía performing arts centre

A beluga whale at the *Oceanogràfic*

along its landscaped pathway. The 42 million litres of water makes the *Oceanogràfic* one of the largest aquariums in Europe; the roof built in the shape of a water lily is the work of the Spanish-Mexican architect Félix Candela. Lastly, the *Palau de les Artes Reina Sofía* is a centre dedicated to music and performing arts. Tourists visiting this grand "city" will enjoy a tour brimming with curiosities. What's more, there are guided tours to get an in-depth look at the architecture or the secrets of the Science Museum.

BASILICA OF THE PILLAR

Legend has it that the Basilica of the Pillar was built around the "pillar" on which the Virgin appeared to St. James the Apostle.

Since 40 AD, when this event supposedly occurred, the basilica has been a site for venerating the "pillar" (a jasper column) from which the Virgin descended in mortal flesh. No historic document or discovery has managed to prove the legend, which was only referred to in a bull from Pope Boniface VIII in 1297.

The church itself dates back to the 9th century, according to the *Historia translationis sancti Vincentii* written by Aimonio, a monk from Saint Germain-des-Prés (Paris), who certified the existence of a Mozarabic temple that stood in this spot devoted to the Virgin Mary. In 1118 Alfonso I of Aragon ordered the rebuilding of the church, which had been in ruins. Another reconstruction was begun in the Gothic-Mudéjar style in 1293 and completed in 1518. In 1681 work began on the Baroque basilica and in 1750 Ventura Rodríguez made some changes which gave it the neoclassical appearance it has today. Between 1796 and 1872, the year the church was considered terminated, the basilica was outfitted with the towers and dome that give it its

Central nave

View of the Basilica of the Pillar and the Ebro River

characteristic shape. Nevertheless, the outer towers, which reach over 90 metres tall, were mostly built in the 20th century and were only finished in 1961.

The exterior of this cathedral-basilica is remarkable for its eleven domes, composed of glazed green, yellow, blue and white roof tiles, and its Romanesque tympanum, the only feature remaining from the medieval church. The interior stands out for its chapel devoted to the Virgin Mary of the Pillar, a small Baroque temple (18th century) designed by Ventura Rodríguez to house the "pillar" on which the Virgin appeared. The image of the Virgin Mary (15th century), a gilded wood carving just 8 centimetres high, is attributed to the sculptor Juan de Huerta.

ALJAFERÍA PALACE

Aljafería Palace is one of the three most important buildings of Islamic art in Spain, along with the Mosque of Cordoba and the Alhambra of Granada.

The rustic outside of this fortified palace with its high walls and tower keeps does not go with the delicate architecture and exquisite decoration of its magnificent interior. Built in the second half of the 11th century by Al-Muqtadir, the king of the *taifa* of Saraqusta (Zaragoza) from 1046 to 1081, it was used as the royal residence of the Banu Hud dynasty. Originally it was called *qasr al-Surur*, or the "Palace of Joy", and its luxurious quarters bear witness to the splendour of this independent kingdom lasting from 1018 to 1110, until it fell into the hands of the Almoravids. The Aljafería Palace is considered the only example of a large Islamic building from the era of the *taifas* still standing today.

The palace's decoration displays a range of elements belonging to Islamic architecture, such as combined arches, springers, arabesques and plasterwork featuring plant motifs. After the reconquest of Zaragoza (1118) by Alfonso I, the palace became the residence

The Throne Room of the Catholic Monarchs

Entrance façade

Arcades of the royal palace

of the Christian kings of Aragon, and from that moment on and in the centuries to come it would undergo a series of renovations. The Catholic Monarchs, for example, erected a fortress atop the Muslim edifice, a project led by Faraig de Gali, Muhammad Monferriz and Muhammad Palacio, master builders of Muslim descent. A special feature of the fortress of the Catholic Monarchs is the magnificent craftsmanship in its Throne Room. After 1485 the palace became the headquarters and prison (the Keep of the Troubadour) of the Inquisition, and in the mid-20th century, the seat of the *Cortes de Aragón*, the Aragon Parliament.

Valderrobres, Teruel

UNIQUE TOWNS AND VILLAGES

CUDILLERO

The seaside village and fishing port of Cudillero is considered among the prettiest in Spain.

The hillside above Cudillero (in Asturian *Cuideiru*) in the hamlet of El Pito is the site of the **Selgas Palace**, the former residence of the magnate and historian Fortunato de Selgas (1838-1921). The palace has a pavilion containing Renaissance tapestries (16th century) and various paintings, such as *Diana cured by Endymion*, by Luca Giordano, an *Ascension* by El Greco and *Hannibal Contemplating Italy for the First Time, From the Alps*, Goya's first ever painting. However, Cudillero's main attraction undoubtedly lies in exploring the steep alleyways of the fishing village, whose vernacular houses line the narrow darkened streets and face towards the sea, their shapes well adapted to the lay of the land.

The village's main points of interest include the 13th-century Chapel of **Cristo del Humilladero**, a square Gothic-style church with buttresses and ogive

The old port

Plaza de la Marina

The new port

vaults whose interior contains altarpieces from the 16th and 17th centuries. Next in importance is **St. Peter's Church**, the patron saint of the village, built in the 16th century thanks to donations from the local residents. The Gothic-style church, with a single nave, semi-circular apse, side chapels and a rib vault, was heavily damaged in the Civil War of 1936-1939. Nevertheless, the interior contains several interesting Baroque pieces, such as carvings of St. Francis and St. Peter by the sculptor Antonio de Borja (1660-1730).

LLANES

Popular among tourists, Llanes offers its visitors all the magic of a small seaside village stuck in a bygone era.

In 1225 King Alfonso IX conceded Llanes a town charter in order to settle the land and better defend it. Later Alfonso X would concede it a new charter, which led to the gradual growth of the town and the walls were built. Between the 13th and 14th centuries, Llanes reached the apex of its economic development. Alfonso XI conceded it a salt depository due to rise of its port, whose ships were trading with Portugal, France and England. However, the Catholic Monarchs revoked this privilege in the 15th century and Llanes entered a period of decline. In 1809, Napoleon's troops, under General Bonnet, entered Llanes and installed their barracks in the Convent of the Augustinian Recollects. During this period, there were constant skirmishes between the

Llanes Marina

Ballota Beach

Cubes of Memory by Agustín Ibarrola

French troops and the local resistance, led by José Balmorí Sánchez. Only a small part of the walls that used to surround Llanes remain, as well as a keep of the fortress built by Alfonso IX. The Church of **St. Mary of the Assumption**, better known as **St. Mary of the Council** (12th century), maintains its original Romanesque structure despite countless renovations, although it is generally considered to be a Gothic building. The **Convent of the Augustinian Recollects**, today a hotel, retains its 17th century portal. The baroque **Palace of the Duke of Estrada** (16th century) features two square towers on each side of its main façade.

LUARCA

A safe harbour for fishermen and a refuge for pilgrims on their way to Santiago, Luarca retains its traditional seafaring districts and a cemetery whose mausolea overlook the sea.

Luarca (in Asturian *Lluarca*), whose most illustrious citizen might be Severo Ochoa, winner of the Nobel Prize in Physiology or Medicine in 1959, is split down the middle by the Negro River. The town gained importance in the whaling days of the 19th century, when its port was among the most important on the Cantabrian Sea. Sailing ships would depart from the port of Luarca to trade with the Americas. The old fishermen's quarters of La Pescadería and El Cambaral are the result of those heydays. The latter is home to the ***Mesa de Mareantes***, the great table around which the Luarca Sailors Guild would hold their gatherings.

The town's main points of interest include its **port** with the multi-coloured hulls of its fishing boats and the eclectic **Town Hall** built between 1912 and

The old port

The port and mouth of the Negro River

1916 with its three-sided façade and art-nouveau attic windows. The **Church of St. Eulalia**, near the port, still has its old stone transept and cemetery. The **churchyard of Luarca**, whose immaculate white mausolea and tombstones are perched atop the **Atalaya** cliffs, is the burial ground of Severo Ochoa. Next to the cemetery is the **Atalaya Chapel**, also known as the **Hermitage of the White Virgin**, which contains some images of Luarca's Holy Week processions.

The cemetery

Nature lovers have an unlimited number of options for walking excursions. They can head to **Cape Busto** or take up the Royal Way of Madrid to Santiago de Compostela, a centuries-old trade and pilgrimage route.

GUADALUPE

This small town of just over two thousand inhabitants contains the Royal Monastery of St. Mary of Guadalupe, considered one of the greatest sights in Extremadura and declared a World Heritage Site by UNESCO.

According to legend, in the late 13th century a local shepherd, later identified as Gil Cordero, discovered an image of the Virgin Mary and built a small hermitage on that very spot. In 1335 Alfonso XI of Castile, the grandson of Alfonso X the Wise, paid a visit and decided to restore the hermitage and enlarge it. A few years later, in 1340, after his victory in the Battle of Río Salado, King Alfonso XI had a monastery built. After a time as a secular priory, which lasted until 1389, the monastery spent five centuries (until the ecclesiastical confiscations of Mendizábal of 1835) under the tutelage of the Order of St. Jerome.

Sacristy with paintings by Zurbarán

The Virgin of Guadalupe in her shrine

The **Monastery** has several noteworthy areas, such as its Gothic basilica and the Mudéjar rose window over its pediment, the main altar with a 17th

The Basilica of Guadalupe

century altarpiece by the Flemish sculptor Giraldo de Merlo, the 17th-century sacristy with eight paintings by Francisco de Zurbarán, and finally the shrine of the Virgin of Guadalupe. The Virgin, a Romanesque image (12th century) cedar carving, is exhibited in an octagonal Baroque camarín designed by Matías Román with nine paintings by Luca Giordano commissioned by Charles II. In addition, the monastery invites visitors into its three museums on **Embroidery**, **Miniature Books** and **Sculpture and Painting**, containing objects such as an embroidery of the Passion (15th century), a book of hours (16th century) and paintings by Zurbarán and Goya, respectively.

TRUJILLO

Trujillo, "the city of the conquistadors", was the birthplace of Francisco Pizarro, the conquistador of Peru, and Francisco de Orellana, discoverer of the Amazon.

The Romans called it Turgalium, which over time became the Mozarabic-influenced Trujillo. Under the Moors, the town had become prosperous, but it reached its maximum splendour after the Christian reconquest by becoming a lordship with jurisdiction over two dozen villages (15th century). John II of Castile, the son of Henry III the Sufferer and Catherine of Lancaster, conceded it the title of "city" (1430), and after the discovery of America, many residents left for the New World to make their fortunes, returning loaded down with riches to erect the palaces and mansions that dot the old quarter.

A relaxing stroll around Trujillo lets you discover its rich artistic heritage. In the Renaissance-era **Plaza**

Plaza Mayor

Cloister in the Pizarro Palace

Mayor, lined with arcades and several 16th-century palaces and noble homes, is a statue of Francisco Pizarro on horseback. The town is overlooked by the **castle**, a fortress built between the 9th and 12th centuries on the hill called *Cabeza de Zorro* (Fox Head). The 16th-century **palace of the *Marqueses de la Conquista*** (the Marquises of the Conquest) was built by Hernando Pizarro and his wife and niece Francisca Pizarro, the daughter of Francisco, the discoverer of Peru, evidenced by the corner balcony decorated with the Pizarro coat of arms. Last but not least of the main monuments of Trujillo is the Romanesque **Church of St. Mary Major** (13th century).

ARCOS DE LA FRONTERA

Perched atop a rock overlooking the Guadalete River, the town of Arcos de la Frontera is dotted with the whitewashed walls of its houses and dominated by its towering parish church.

St. Peter's Church

According to legend, the foundation of Arcos is the work of King Brigo, the grandson of Noah, which is why in antiquity Arcos was known by the name of *Arcobrigan*. However, historians disagree with the legend and insist that the name is of Arabic origin, from *ar*, *arci*, meaning "fortress". The Moors called it Arkus and made it the administrative seat of one of the *taifa* kingdoms (11th century). After the conquest of Seville (1248) by Ferdinand the Saint, Arcos de la Frontera was annexed to Castile, although Muslims were allowed to keep their homes. In 1264, there was a revolt in Lower Andalusia, and Arcos once more fell into the hands of the *Saracens* until Alfonso X the Wise conquered it for good and expelled the Saracens.

Street in the old quarter

In 1962, the beauty of Arcos de la Frontera caused its old quarter to be declared an Artistic-Historic Monument, both for its heritage and the labyrinth of streets and alleyways of the old quarter. A stroll through it leads to the **Casa Espinosa**, one of the oldest façades of a civil building in Andalusia. The

Arcos de la Frontera

religious architecture stands out for the **Church of St. Mary of the Assumption** (16th century), which is accessed up an 18th century staircase that leads to its Flamboyant Gothic façade (16th century). The interior contains various treasures, such as the main altarpiece by Jerónimo Hernández and Andrés Ocampo, the Baroque choir and retroquire, magnificent frescoes, particularly the one dedicated to the *Coronation of the Virgin Mary*, a painting from the Siena school, important Baroque altarpieces, such as the one in the Chapel of the Snows with the image of its namesake Virgin, and certain architectural solutions that demonstrate the mastery of its craftsmanship, such as the dome of the Baptism Chapel. **St. Peter's Church**, which contains the oldest altarpiece in the province of Cadiz with paintings by Pacheco, Zurbarán and Ribera, was built in the Flamboyant Gothic style with features of both the Renaissance and Baroque. The **castle** was used as the residence of the dukes of Arcos until the noble line died out. Moorish in origin but renovated in the 14th and 15th centuries, it was in this castle that the Catholic Monarchs received word that the *taifa* of Marbella had surrendered. The **Convent of St. Francis** retains a fascinating tile daco with the stations of the cross. Finally, the **Chapel of Charity** (14th century) is one of the first buildings in Andalusia designed in the Colonial style (17th century).

SANTILLANA DEL MAR

It is considered one of Spain's most beautiful and oldest towns, as it was documented in 980 under the name of Planes.

The name Santillana comes from the founding of its basilica dedicated to Sancta Iuliana, or St. Juliana, a young girl from Nicomedia (Turkey) martyred in Asia Minor during the persecutions decreed by Emperor Diocletian at the end of the 3rd century and whose remains were brought to Spain in the 9th century.

Merino Tower

Santo Domingo Street

The old quarter of Santillana del Mar is full of neat houses festooned with coats of arms and other examples of traditional architecture rising out of the population boom brought about by the town being made the capital of the regional bailiff, the *Merindad de las Asturias de Santillana*. Most of the town's buildings were erected between the 14th and 17th centuries on and around Santo Domingo Street.

Collegiate Church of St. Juliana

The main monuments of Santillana include the **Valdivieso Palace** (18th century), now a hotel; the **Arenas** or **Velarde Palace** (15th century), built in a transitional style between the Gothic and Renaissance with a façade decorated by pinnacles; the aforementioned Romanesque **Collegiate Church of St. Juliana** (12th century); the **Quevedo and Cossío houses** (17th and 18th century) near the collegiate church and both bearing coats of arms; the **House of the Archduchess** known as **Casa Abades** (17th century), whose coats of arms belonged to the Barreda Bracho family and were sculpted by the contemporary sculptor Jesús Otero; and the **Casa de la Villa (Town Hall)** known as **Casa de los Hombrones**.

ALTAMIRA MUSEUM

Discovered about two kilometres from Santillana del Mar (1868), this cave contains some of the most important prehistoric rock paintings in the world. Altamira Cave, which takes its name from the fields where it was found, was first studied by the palaeontologist and archaeologist Marcelino Sanz de Sautuola, and after much dispute, its paintings and engravings were described as "the Sistine Chapel of Prehistoric Art" due to their spectacular artwork and interest to science.

General view of the Polychrome Room of the Neo-Cave

The paintings of Altamira belong to two main well-defined periods: the Magdalenian (the last higher Palaeolithic culture) and the Solutrean (the upper-middle Palaeolithic), although there are others that correspond to the Gravettian and even the Aurignacian, as has been proven by uranium dating. It can safely be said from these records that the cave had been inhabited for 22,000 years until the cave entrance collapsed.

The style of these paintings falls in the Franco-Cantabrian school, characterised by the realism of the figures, particularly the animals and anthropomorphic beings. The animal most often depicted in the cave is the European bison *(Bison bonasus)* painted in various sizes and postures with 16 multi-coloured versions and one in black. To paint the figures, the artist or artists first selected their space and then outlined the contours, first in black and then adding the other colours.

The original cave was closed to the public (September 2002) to protect the paintings from the deterioration brought on by years of visitors, but the Altamira Museum was soon opened with a permanent exhibition which includes a meticulously exact three-dimensional reproduction of its famous Polychrome Room, plus laboratories, a library, shop, etc. This museum, a kind of neo-cave, allows you to discover the lives of the Palaeolithic humans who painted their famous bison. The museum rooms are devoted to the art and culture of Palaeolithic hunter-gatherers.

Bison in the Polychrome Room

PEÑÍSCOLA

The beaches and coves of Peñíscola attract thousands of holidaymakers every year who thoroughly enjoy themselves in this village that seems stuck in time.

The Arabs built the first fortress that Knights Templar would later expand and reinforce after the reconquest of Peñíscola, turning it into a vitally important bastion in the defence of this stretch of coastline. Over time, the town's population dwindled to the size of a small fishing village, and it was not until two films were shot there, *Calabuch* (1956) by Luis García Berlanga, and *El Cid* (1962) by Anthony Mann, that it was put squarely on the international tourist map and the first visitors began to stream in.

Perched atop a peninsula and joined to the mainland by a tombolo (a land spit), the **Templar castle** (13th century) was built by Friar Berenguer of Cardona, the master builder of the Templar Order in Catalonia and Aragon, and Friar Arnaldo of Banyuls, commendator of Peñíscola, whose coats of arms can still be seen above its entrance gate. The Templar castle, built

The old town and port

The Templar Castle, or the Castle of Papa Luna

Artillery Battery of the Bufador

of solid stone blocks underwent a thorough renovation when it became the residence of Benedict XIII, known as the *Papa Luna* in Spanish and now considered an anti-pope. Later, on the orders of Philip II, its walls were adapted for heavy artillery to repel the attempts to take control of the town by enemy ships, some of them pirates. The task fell to the Italian military architect Giovanni Battista Antonelli, who carried out the works between 1576 and 1578. The castle architecture stands out for its robust walls which rise vertically from the edges of the small cliffs of the peninsula, and the barrel-vaulted rooms built by the Templar knights.

ALMAGRO

Almagro's medieval architecture makes the village one of the top tourist attractions in Castile-La Mancha.

The first mention of the city of Almagro was in a document attributed to Alfonso VIII dated 1176. In Roman times, the area was an important crossroads on the Toledo-Castulo road, which branched off in Calatrava la Vieja towards Almagro and connected up with the *Vía de la Plata* (the Silver Way) crossing the Sierra Morena mountains. Various historians believe Almagro was founded next to a bridge that was built on the orders of the Archbishop of Toledo. The bridge was called the "Miracle" (*al-Milagro*, in Arabic) which became corrupted into Almagro. In 1222, Almagro became the seat of the Order of Calatrava and entered a period of splendour that led to the building of several monasteries, churches, inns, etc. The fame of Almagro in those days can be seen in

Plaza Mayor

Corral de Comedias

the arrival of such figures as the Fuggers, a family of German businessmen and bankers, the Gedlers, who ran the Almadén mines, and the Welsers, a family of Hapsburg bankers.

The most remarkable feature of Almagro is its somewhat irregular **Plaza Mayor**, whose Tuscan columns uphold arcades with two levels of enclosed verandas used to seat the audience during the events taking place in the

Gedler Palace

square (its current appearance dates from the 17th century). On one side of the square there is the **Corral de Comedias**, a medieval theatre declared a monument in 1995. It is in the former inn on the square, the *Posada de las Comedias* and hosted performances of the works of Cervantes, Tirso de Molina, Lope and Calderón. Finally, just off the square is the **Maestral Palace**, with a 14th-century Mudéjar cloister featuring horseshoe arches.

FIGUERES

Capital of the Alt Empordà region, Figueres finds its roots in a medieval village belonging to the County of Besalú.

The first historical documents referring to Figueres date back to the 10th century. However, it was first populated in 600 BC, as evidenced by the archaeological remains of an Iberian settlement belonging to the Indigetes tribe that was discovered in the Muntanyeta, the hill currently occupied by the

Museum of the Empordà

St. Ferdinand's Castle

St. Ferdinand's Castle. Later it was the Romans who had disembarked in Emporion that established a small village by the name of Joncaria, due to the abundance of *juncos* (rushes). In 802 it was known as Villa Ficerias and the first document mentioning Figueres (Figariae) dates from 962. In 1111 it became part of the County of Barcelona and on 21st June 1267, James I the Conqueror gave it a town charter, which came with various privileges. It took on its current appearance in the 19th century, although it would be heavily bombed in the Spanish Civil War of 1936-1939.

In the centre of the old part of Figueres is **Gala-Dalí Square**, the location of one of the most visited museums in Spain, the **Dalí Theatre-Museum**. Occupying the former municipal theatre (19th century) that had been destroyed in the Spanish Civil War, the museum contains several works of this world-renowned

Galatea Tower, the Dalí Museum

painter whose mortal remains also lie here, rather against his wishes (Dalí preferred Púbol Castle). The collections cover a wide range of Dalí's work, from his early artistic expressions to the last years of his life. Some of the best pieces include *Girl from Figueres* (1926), *Soft Self-Portrait with Grilled Bacon* (1941), *The Basket of Bread* (1945) and *Napoleon's Nose, Transformed into a Pregnant Woman, Strolling His Shadow with Melancholia amongst Original Ruins* (1945). On the other side of the square is **St. Peter's Church**, which still preserves some of its Romanesque features from the 12th and 13th centuries.

There are two other museums in Figueres which draw thousands of visitors: the **Museum of the Empordà** and the **Toy Museum**. The former contains sculptures by Frederic Marès, objects of local archaeology and works from various artists of the Empordà region from the 19th and 20th centuries. The latter has a collection of over three thousand toys.

SIGÜENZA

Sigüenza, a strategic crossroads throughout the Middle Ages, was once Segontia, a city in Celtiberia mentioned by Pliny the Elder.

Previously inhabited by the Arevaci tribe, Sigüenza was conquered by the Romans after the fall of Numantia (133 BC) and they turned it into an important trading town along the Henares consul route forming part of the network of roads between Mérida (Emerita Augusta) and Zaragoza (Caesar Augusta). The Moors built the **castle**, today a *Parador*, a state-run historic hotel, which for centuries was the home of the local bishop.

The Cathedral of **St. Mary Major** (12th century) honours the patron saint of Sigüenza, Mary Major, and was built in the Cistercian Romanesque style with some Gothic features added at a later date. Inside, the Chapel of Los Arce is the site of the famous tomb of Martín Vázquez de Arce (1461-1486), better known as the "*Doncel* of Sigüenza", meaning "young noble-

Cathedral of St. Mary Major

man", a Castilian officer and aristocrat who died in the war against Granada. His perfectly carved tomb is considered one of the most important Gothic sculptures in Spain. The old quarter of Sigüenza contains several other interesting churches, such as the Romanesque church dedicated to **St. James the Apostle**, built during the pontificate of Bishop Cerebruno (1156-1167). The church forms part of the convent of the Poor Clares, who abandoned it in the 1940s in favour of the Alameda. The former convent has now become a private residence. **St. Vincent's Church** (12th century), in the heart of the medieval city, contains a remarkable polychrome carving of the crucified Christ (12th or 13th century). The 16th-century **Church of Our Lady of the Orchard**, on the fertile plain of the Henares River, was built in the Renaissance-Gothic style with Plateresque decoration. Its portal is decorated with a three-centred arch, while the top of the façade con-

The House of the *Doncel*

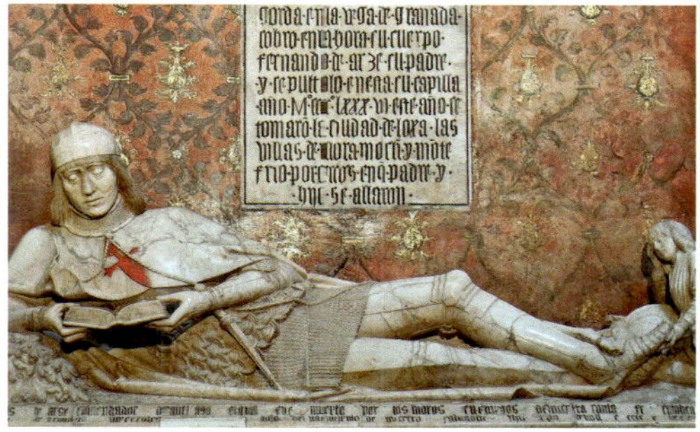

The *Doncel* of Sigüenza

tains gargoyles and flying buttresses. The **Convent of St. Francis** (17th century), currently inhabited by the sisters of St Ursula, still bears the Franciscan coat of arms in various parts of its façade. Franciscan monks were installed in the convent until the ecclesiastical confiscations of Mendizábal (1835).

An example of the town's secular architecture can be found in the neighbourhood of San Roque: the Baroque **Palacio de los Infantes** (Palace of the Children), by the master builder Bernascono, which was once home to the Escolanía de los Infantes, a music school for the cathedral boys' choir. The chief feature is its grand portal, decorated by a frieze containing various sculptures and a statue of St. Philip Neri standing in a niche. The only thing left of the Renaissance-style **palace** on Cardenal Mendoza Street is its Plateresque portal bearing the coat of arms of Bishop Fadrique de Portugal. It is believed to have hosted the court of the Inquisition.

ARANJUEZ

At the confluence of the Tagus and Jarama rivers, Aranjuez became a Royal Site of the Crown of Spain at the behest of King Philip II.

Aranjuez is famous throughout Spain for its Royal Palace and Gardens, but it is also known across the globe thanks to Joaquín Rodrigo of Valencia, the composer who, although blinded by diphtheria, wrote the *Concierto de Aranjuez* in 1939, considered the most frequently performed piece of Spanish music in the world.

The **Royal Palace** of Aranjuez, the residence of the royal family, is situated on the banks of the Tagus River amidst its leafy Renaissance-style **gardens**. It owes its construction to Philip II, who commissioned the design and work to the architect Juan Bautista de Toledo. Bautista's death before the project's conclusion meant Juan de Herrera had to step in. Work ground to a halt in the 17th century and would only recommence in the times of Ferdinand VI. Charles III ultimately decided upon the architectural style that can be seen in the palace today.

Royal Palace and gardens

Main façade of the Royal Palace

The chief features of the interior include the main staircase and the Guard Room, which contain paintings by Luca Giordano, olive wood and bronze furniture and Imperial French vases. The Queen's Room contains works by Giordano and Vicente Carducho, while the Mirror Room was decorated by Luca Giordano. As for the gardens, they are irrigated by the waters of the Tagus and the Jarama rivers and considered the most important of the Spanish Hapsburg period.

Near the palace at one end of the Prince's Garden stands the **Casa del Labrador** (the Farmhand's House), built in the 18th century by Juan de Villanueva. Charles IV commissioned Villanueva to build a small palace. He took advantage of a former farmhouse, and even then the work still lasted from 1790 to 1803. The 3-level slate-roofed mansion is richly decorated on the exterior, whose niches contain their corresponding classical statures, plus floral and putti reliefs, and the busts of famous Greco-Romans. The best of its lavishly decorated interior (stuccoes, bronzes, solid wood, marble and glass) is undoubtedly the ballroom which has been draped in silk with Pompeii motifs, glass chandeliers and Sèvres vases and amphorae.

The **Jardín del Príncipe** (the Prince's Garden), near a pier, contains the **Museum of Royal Feluccas**,

STRAWBERRY TRAIN

On 9th February 1851, the country's second rail line was opened which united Madrid and Aranjuez, not too long after the Barcelona-Mataró train was put into service (1848).

The original purpose of the Madrid railway was to eventually connect the capital with the port of Alicante. In addition, the Spanish monarchy, embodied at that time by Isabella II, was keen on the idea of making it quicker to travel between two of its residences, the royal palaces of Madrid and Aranjuez; the 49-kilometre train journey only took an hour and a half.

The railway that joined Madrid and Aranjuez soon became known as the "*tren de la fresa*" or the Strawberry Train, due to the many farmers along the fertile banks of the Tagus who used it to take their goods, principally strawberries and asparagus, to Madrid's markets. These days, the Strawberry Train makes special runs during spring and autumn (Saturdays, Sundays and public holidays).

Strawberry Train

Pond of Los Chinescos, the Prince's Garden

The Jardín de la Isla Garden

rebuilt in 1966 by the architect Ramón Andrade. The museum has a collection of the country's most important Spanish royal vessels in the country. Used by the kings of Spain to ply up and down the Tagus, these vessels are richly adorned with gold-leaf carvings and wood filigree, restored to all their splendour. The most remarkable of all is the felucca that belonged to Charles IV, built in the shipyards of Cartagena and decorated by the renowned court painter Mariano Salvador Maella in 1774; a close second is the gondola of Philip V, handed down since the times of Charles II (17th century).

CHINCHÓN

Several cultures have left their mark on the town, judging by its many sights.

The Chinchón of today dates from 1498, when the locals had to abandon the plains due to a plague of mosquitoes and move to the top of a hill, currently the site of the church of **Our Lady of the Assumption** . Built between 1534 and 1616, initially by Alonso de Covarrubias, the church was once the chapel for the comital palace. To build the church, Diego Fernández de Cabrera, the Count of Chinchón and majordomo of Philip II, hired the best master builders who had worked on the monastery of San Lorenzo de El Escorial. In 1808, during the Peninsular War, Napoleon's soldiers set fire to it and other buildings in the town, and also killed 86 local residents in revenge for the deaths of two French soldiers. The church's main altarpiece is presided by *The Assumption of the Virgin Mary*, a painting by Francisco de Goya in 1812. Next to the church is the popular **Clock Tower** (15th century), which used to be part of the former parish church of Our Lady of Grace, destroyed by the French. However, the main attraction of Chinchón is undoubtedly its main square.

The **Plaza Mayor** of Chinchón is considered a fine example of the traditional architecture found in

Plaza Mayor with the Church of Our Lady of the Assumption

Arcades of the Plaza Mayor

Typical Castilian balconies

Castilian squares of the Middle Ages. Its first houses, with their balconies and galleries and the straight bases and footings of their wood beam arcades, were built in the 15th century, although the entire perimeter of the square as it is seen today would not be completed until the 17th century. The square has been the site of mock spear fights, royal and popular festivals, bullfights, theatrical performances, inquisitorial public penances, executions and countless other spectacles. Today the square is home to numerous restaurants, bars and shops selling regional products, such as local garlic and *anís de Chinchón*, an anisette liqueur with a reputation for quality.

SAN LORENZO DE EL ESCORIAL

Every year thousands of tourists come to this Madrilenian municipality to visit the Royal Monastery of San Lorenzo de El Escorial, at the foot of Mount Abantos on the south-eastern slopes of the Guadarrama Mountains.

The town of El Escorial, founded in the epoch of Charles III, became a municipality in the 19th century. Its fame, however, dates back to the 14th century when Philip II, during the festivals of St. Lawrence, ordered the building of a grand monastery to commemorate his victory in the Battle of St. Quentin (1557). The building, whose construction spanned from 1563 to 1584, was given over to the Hieronymites, although today it is run by the monks of the Order of St. Augustine. The complex consists of a palace, which is an official residence of the royal family, and a basilica, whose mausoleum contains the mortal remains of the monarchs of Spain.

The monastery and the other buildings are spread over an area of 33,327 m^2 and it is considered the most important Renaissance monument in Spain and one of the best in Europe. Began by Juan Bautista de Toledo (c. 1515-1567), who died before it could be completed, the design was handed over to his disciple Juan de Herrera, who finished it on 13th September 1584.

The design's complexity, both in terms of its size and the technical measures that were adopted, has put the monastery in a significant position on the timeline of Spanish architecture, marking the transition between the Plateresque style of the Renaissance and forthcoming Classicism. In 1984, on the fourth centennial of the commencement of the work, UNESCO included the Royal Monastery of San Lorenzo de El Escorial, as well as other royal buildings such as the Houses of the

Main façade

Library

Prince and the Infante, on its list of World Heritage Sites.

Among the most noteworthy areas of this sprawling monastic and palatial complex is the Library, designed by Juan de Herrera, with a superb barrel vault decorated with frescoes depicting the seven liberal arts – Rhetoric, Dialectic, Music, Grammar, Arithmetic, Geometry and Astrology – each painted by Pellegrino Tibaldi according to the iconographic scheme approved by Father Sigüenza. The Library contains a trove of books on clock making, cosmography, medicine, descriptions of exotic countries, a manuscript on the life and travels of Hernán Cortes, and countless classics by Homer, Ovid, Aristophanes and Pliny. The frescoes in the Hall of Battles, a gallery 60 metres long and 8 metres high, depict some of the great battles involving Spanish troops, such as the Battle of St. Quentin.

The crypt, built by Juan Gómez de Mora according to the plans of Juan Bautista Crescenzi, is presided by a

Sculpture of Philip II and his family in prayer, Pompeo Leoni

The Monastery from the pastures of the Dehesa de la Herrería

large crucifix by Pietro Tacca and contains twenty-six marble tombs with the mortal remains of the kings and queens of the houses of Austria and Bourbon, with a few notable exceptions (Philip V, buried in the Palace of La Granja de San Ildefonso in Segovia, and Ferdinand VI, who lies in the Salesas Reales in Madrid).

According to Friar Antonio de Villacastín, the church's great ribbed arch was enclosed on 4th April 1579, and a short time later, the first chapel. The first Mass was held on 18th May 1584 on the altar of St. Anne, while the last stone was placed in the cornice of the courtyard on 13th September 1584.

Lastly, it is worth mentioning the Palace of the Austrias, built around the basilica presbytery, according to the model of Charles I's in Yuste. The bedrooms reflect the austerity the king required of his quarters. During his lengthy illness Philip II could hear Mass from his bed. The doors contain a surprisingly amount of detail, as do the hundreds of religious objects on display, including crucifixes, ivory carvings of the life of Christ, and a Virgin Mary by Carracci, to name just a few. The only areas open to the public are the royal quarters, the Library and the Hall of Battles.

Southern façade of the Monastery

FRIGILIANA

Nestled between the Almijara Mountains and the Mediterranean, this town in the heart of the Axarquía region of Malaga has all the look of a typical southern village on the peninsula.

The caves and rock shelters of Frigiliana were the refuge of Neolithic man, and would later bear witness to Phoenicians, who left behind a Punic necropolis, and then the Romans, Visigoths and the Moors. These cultures all left their mark on Frigiliana, in vestiges great or small, such as its **castle**, destroyed (1569) by the Christian troops led by Luis de Requesens, a general from Barcelona who crushed the fleeing Moriscos after the Revolt of the Alpujarras. Since 1982 his deeds have been displayed on the colourful tile panels that decorate the town's streets.

A stroll through Frigiliana leads to hidden alleyways adorned with flower-filled clay pots which add a dash of spring and summer colour to the town's

A street in Frigiliana

Frigiliana as seen from the Mudéjar quarter

Frigiliana

whitewashed walls and wooden doors. Clambering up and down the steep hills, you come across its manor houses, such as the Renaissance-style residence of the **Manrique de Lara** family (16th century), the *Casa de Los Condes;* **St. Anthony's Church**, built in the Renaissance style in 1676 with a Latin cross and three naves, and the **Hermitage of the Holy Christ of the Cane**, (18th century). Its main point of interest, however, is the **Archaeological Museum of Frigiliana**, whose collections trace the history of Frigiliana found in the main archaeological sites located in the municipality. Its most important object is perhaps the "*Niño de Frigiliana*", a child's cranium from the Neolithic period.

NERJA

The easternmost town in the county of Axarquía has become an important centre for tourism in the province of Malaga.

Founded by the Moors, who called it *Narixa*, from which the town gets its name, Nerja is home to the famous **Nerja Cave**, discovered in 1959 and a refuge for the prehistoric humans who colonised this part of the Mediterranean coast, evidenced by the rock paintings they left behind.

Nerja Cave, the Room of the Cataclysm, lower galleries

The Balcony of Europe

Near the village of Maro, a hamlet in the municipality of Nerja, the cave has been adapted for tourists and consists of two sections: one open to the public and the other restricted. All in all, there are 5 kilometres of explored caves which have several karst formations (stalactites, stalagmites, columns, flowstones, etc.). The interior contains the world's thickest natural column (*Guinness Book of Records*, 1989), a formation where a stalactite and a stalagmite come together. However, the most remarkable aspect of the cave is undoubtedly its rock paintings, archaeological sites and strata dating from 20,000 to 3,600 years ago. The paintings were made by the Neanderthals, a species in the *Homo* genus who inhabited Europe and parts of Western Asia during the upper and middle Pleistocene.

The centre of Nerja is home to the **Balcony of Europe**, an excellent spot for enjoying fantastic views of the Mediterranean judging by the throngs of tourists at sunset. An old Arab fort stood on the spot in the 9th century. The name "Balcony of Europe" was actually coined by King Alfonso XII on a visit to Nerja (1885) after an earthquake had caused serious damage to the town. Near this peculiar "balcony" is the **Nerja History Museum**, whose collection contains objects discovered in and around the town. One of its more noteworthy pieces is the complete skeleton known as "Pepita", which is around 8,000 years old. The **Aqueduct of Águila** (19th century) was built to transport water to run the former San Joaquín de Maro sugar mills. The aqueduct's four levels formed by superimposed arches reach high enough to span the Coladilla ravine. The baroque-style **Hermitage of the Sorrows** (17th century) still retains a small bell-gable and several frescoes inside its dome believed to belong to the Granada school of Alonso Cano. Inside there is also a statue of Our Lady of Sorrows, the patron saint of the town of Nerja. The **Church of Our Saviour** (17th century), part Mudéjar and part Baroque, has a square tower topped by an octagonal bell tower. Inside are several murals painted by Francisco Hernández, and straight opposite the church is a large monkey puzzle tree brought from South America in 1887.

This area of the coast was home to many sugar mills, and a few still remain, such as the **Ingenio de San Antonio Abad**. In addition, the coast of Nerja has some excellent beaches that attract a great number of sunbathers in summertime. **Burriana** (800 metres long) and **Chuco** (200 metres long) beaches are among the best, not to mention **Torrecilla** Beach (300 metres long).

Horse-drawn carriages at the Balcony of Europe

RONDA

Located in the county of Serranía de Ronda, the town extends over a broad plateau called the "depression of Ronda".

Ronda, one of the oldest cities in Spain, can trace its origins back to Neolithic times as evidenced by several archaeological finds discovered in its old quarter, although the presence of humans in the area actually dates from the Palaeolithic epoch given the rock paintings of the Cave of La Pileta, some of the best examples found in Andalusia. The Romans settled in the town, which had already been inhabited by Iber tribes, and gave it the name of Arunda. The Visigoths also left their mark on the area, but it would be the Moors who truly gave it its character, turning the small village into a regional capital and a defensive bastion over the roads leading to Lower Andalusia.

The old town is divided into three neighbourhoods: **San Francisco**, the oldest and location of the fortress;

Ronda Bridge

The Bullring

View of El Tajo Canyon

Mercadillo, founded after the reconquest and home to a cluster of Baroque buildings whose windows contain fine examples of the local ironwork; and finally the charming neighbourhood of **Ciudad**, where the most important palaces, churches and convents were built.

The many different points of interest include the **Convent of Santo Domingo** (15th century), whose church contains a polychrome Mudéjar framework roof. The **bullring** (18th century), property of the Real Maestranza de Caballería of Ronda, is considered the oldest and largest in the world. Its 66-metre diameter area is surrounded by 5 rows of seats with 136 columns to form the arches. The **Church of St. Mary Major** (15th century), built atop the Muslim mosque on the orders of the Catholic Monarchs, contains a two-level choir carved in walnut and cedar and stalls adorned with the litanies of the Virgin Mary and the Sacred Heart, as well as an altarpiece devoted to the Our Lady of Sorrows whose image is attributed to Martínez Montañés or La Rolcana, a sculptress from Seville. Lastly, a picture of Ronda would not be complete without its 18th-century **New Bridge**, 98 metres high and built of stone blocks.

BAIONA

This seaside town near Vigo, thanks to its fine beaches and excellent gastronomy, became an important 19th-century holiday resort.

According to legend, Julius Caesar reached Baiona in the year 60 with a fleet to subdue the Herminios, a Lusitani tribe which had taken refuge in the Siccae (Cíes) Islands after being expelled from the Mons Herminius (the Serra da Estrela mountains in modern Portugal). King Alfonso IX of León gave the former Erizana a new name, Baiona, thus dissociating it from the Monastery of St. Mary of Oia and the town enjoyed a period of growth. During the 14th century, it endured attacks from both Portuguese and English corsairs. In 1425 John II granted Baiona and A Coruña a *fuero*, a kind of charter that allowed them to import and export goods.

Monterreal Castle, built between the 12th and 16th centuries, became the main defensive bastion along the estuary inlets known as the Rías Baixas. However,

Monterreal Castle

Baiona

Baiona would truly enter Spanish history books in 1493, when Martín Alonso Pinzón landed on its shores after his return from the Americas. Baiona thus became the first town in Europe to hear the news about the discovery of the New World. To commemorate the arrival, the "Festival of *La Arribada*" is celebrated here in the first week of March. Baiona was raided by pirate ships throughout the 16th century, especially those captained by Francis Drake, who squared off against the troops of the Count of Gondomar in the Bay of Baiona, who managed to defeat them and force them to flee.

The old town, whose century-old white houses with their beautiful glass galleries look out towards the sea, contains some of Baiona's most interesting monuments for visitors. They include the aforementioned castle, now a state-run *parador* hotel; the ***Casa del Perdón*** (House of Forgiveness), named for a chain hung at the entrance which would exempt whoever managed to grasp it from their crimes, by the grace of their majesties, the Catholic Monarchs; the ***Casa de Correa*** (1757), today the city hall; the **Hospital of the Sancti Spiritus** (16th century) now a cultural centre; and the Romanesque **Ex-Collegiate Church of St. Mary** (13th century) with its three naves and rectangular apses. The entrance stands out for its columns and archivolts.

TUI

The area of Tui has been inhabited since prehistoric times, evidenced by the Palaeolithic remains discovered in its fluvial terraces.

Tui is located atop a small promontory. Palaeolithic remains from its first settlers have been discovered on the fluvial terraces of the Miño and Louro rivers. In the times of the Castro culture, it was the capital of the Grovii, a Galician, pre-Roman and Roman people who occupied an area from the valley and mouth of the Miño to the Cíes Islands and the Vigo estuary. In 137 it was colonised by the Romans and classical authors speak of the existence of Castellum Tude and the foundation of the city by Diomedes the Greek, the son of the hero Tydeus (hence the name of Tui). In the early 8th century the area was invaded by the Moors, but it was swiftly retaken in 739 by Alfonso I. In the 12th century, with the independence of the Kingdom of Portugal, Tui became strategically vital and Ferdinand II built its defensive walls in 1170.

Houses with glassed-in galleries

Cathedral portal

Its chief monument is **St. Mary's Cathedral**, whose first stone was laid in 1120. Romanesque in style, it has undergone several redesigns which result in its current Gothic appearance, whose purest form can be found on the façade built in 1225. Another point of interest is the **Diocese Museum and Historical Archive**, a former hospital for the poor and pilgrims built in 1756, which is arranged around a Baroque-style courtyard. The museum collection mostly contains archaeological objects, sacred art and precious metalwork, the latter by silversmiths from Spain and the Americas. The **Convent** and **Church of the Poor Clares**, also called ***Las Encerradas*** (the Confined), dates from 1524 and stands on the site of the former Romanesque church of St. Mary. The current building is the result of the refurbishment, renovation and expansion carried out between the 17th and 18th centuries. Its main asset is undoubtedly its Baroque altarpiece (17th century). **St. Francis's Church** (17th century), which used to be part of the convent of the same name and is now a public library, contains a main altarpiece from the 18th century.

CIUDAD RODRIGO

Just a few kilometres from the Portuguese border, Ciudad Rodrigo was founded on a crossroads that was vital in both peace and war.

Its origins can be traced back to an ancient Vetton fort that some historians associate with the town of Mirobriga. The Romans conquered it and their presence can be found in the three monumental columns forming part of the city's coat of arms, as well as other vestiges of lesser importance. Count Rodrigo, who gave the town its name, attempted to repopulate the area on the orders of Alfonso VI, but it was not until 1161 when Ferdinand II of León managed to carry out the task by turning the town into a strategic point of defence of his territory against the Moors. The walls still surrounding the town date from that period. The 15th and 16th centuries brought great economic wealth to Ciudad Rodrigo and several religious and civil buildings were built, which lend it a rather noble air.

St. James's Gate

The fine preservation of the old quarter earned Ciudad Rodrigo its declaration as a Historic-Artistic Site (1944). One of its more striking monuments is **St. Mary's Cathedral** (12th to 14th centuries), whose Romanesque to Gothic construction was begun under the reign of Ferdinand II of León. The cathedral tower was erected between 1764 and 1770. The 12th-century walls, with a perimeter of over 2 kilometres, are formed by an inner section of stone and mortar, also built in the times of Ferdinand II, and an outer section containing 18 sandstone bastions (18th century) and 5 gates (named the Sun, the Count, Amayuelas, St. James and the Holy Spirit). The Renaissance-style **City Hall** (16th century) underwent a major expansion in 1903 (the right wing). The Herrenian-style **Cerralbo Chapel** (16th and 17th centuries), with a walnut altarpiece (17th century) by local artist Alonso de Balbás, was built as the funeral mausoleum for the Pacheco family, thanks to special authorisation from Cardinal Pacheco of Toledo after the cathedral chapter refused to demolish part of its main chapel to convert it into an ambulatory for the family's mausoleum. The **Church of St. Peter and St. Isidore** (12th century), with its Romanesque-Mudéjar apse, underwent various redesigns in the 16th,

Ciudad Rodrigo and the Tower Keep in the distance

St. Mary's Cathedral

18th and 19th centuries in order to accommodate the funeral mausolea for the city's leading families, such as the Vázquezes, who financed the main chapel of the cathedral and donated the *Virgin Mary of Guadalupe*, an oil painting by the Mexican artist Juan Correa. The **Hospital of the Passion**, founded by the Catholic Monarchs to attend the needy, contains a chapel with a *Crucifixion* by Lucas Mitata (16th century), a sculptor who had worked in several dioceses of the former Kingdom of León. This Christ figure forms part of a Calvary by Juan de Remesal which contains the figures of St. John and the Virgin Mary. Lastly, it is worth mentioning the Renaissance-style **Ávila y Tiedra Palace**.

LA ALBERCA

The pre-Roman fort hidden beneath most of the town streets is evidence of just how long it has been inhabited, yet it still has the appearance of a rural mountain town in the Sierra de Francia mountains.

La Alberca, whose name means "place of water" (derived from the Hebrew *bereka* and the Arabic article *al*), contains a very well-preserved old quarter whose streets are paved in rounded stones and slabs and flanked by traditional houses with wooden framework façades that create intricate geometrical compositions. Its fine state of preservation caused La Alberca to be declared a Historic-Artistic Monument in 1940, making it the first town in Spain to receive such a distinction.

In the Middle Ages, King Alfonso IX of León ordered the resettlement of the land around La Alberca and some of the colonists who came were from France, thanks to Raymond of Burgundy, a French noble married to Lady Urraca, the king's mother. This would explain the large number of French place

Streets and typical houses

Plaza Mayor

names in the Sierra de Francia mountains. At the end of the Middle Ages an important event occurred in the area: the image of Our Lady of Peñafrancia was discovered (15th century), whose sanctuary became a pilgrimage site for those travelling the Way of St. James along the Silver Way. In the 17th century, the importance of the Sierra de Francia mountains and its Black Virgin was such that even Miguel de Cervantes mentioned it in his novel *The Ingenious Gentleman Don Quixote of La Mancha*.

The lintels of the houses of La Alberca are engraved with the date of their construction, an *Ave María* and the symbol of the Inquisition, a palm leaf and a sword, to represent the faith of their occupants. The 18th-century **Church of Our Lady of the Assumption**, built over a much more modestly designed place of worship, stands out for its stout tower, a polychrome granite pulpit (16th century) and, on the outside, a niche containing two human skulls lit up by two lamps, reminding local residents of the brevity of life, the proximity of death, and the need to have one's soul at peace. Visitors who wander the streets of La Alberca may come across the pig of San Antón, who lives in complete freedom and is fed by the locals until the day he is raffled off.

LA GRANJA DE SAN ILDEFONSO

The municipality of La Granja de San Ildefonso in Segoviais famous for its Royal Palace and its monumental gardens.

The name of this former royal summer home comes from an old farm (*granja*) run by Hieronymite monks from their monastery in El Parral (Segovia). In 1724 Philip V retired to the Palace of La Granja and for the next twenty years he would have the gardens arranged and the buildings enlarged.

The interior of the **Palace** contains frescoed vaults, 17th and 19th century paintings and furniture, the Lacquerware Room and a tapestry museum. However, it is the Palace **Gardens** (18th century) which are most renowned thanks to the great forests and parterres designed by the French architect and landscape designer René Carlier. The sequoias which today rise before the Royal Collegiate Church were planted in the 19th century. Amidst the lush vegetation of the gardens there are grand fountains decorated with lead sculptures painted to imitate bronze. Some of the more noteworthy include the fountain of Neptune, Apollo and Andromeda and the Amphitrite waterfall, plus the Eight Lanes, Baths of Diana, and Fame fountains. The water which supplies them comes from a large reservoir.

East façade of the Royal Palace

Fountain of the Three Graces

PEDRAZA

This village still retains its medieval street plan, protected by a castle and towering walls.

The town, possibly of Roman origins, came into being when Fernando Gómez de Albornoz, the high commander of Montalbán, was ordained the Lord of Pedraza by the grace of Henry II of Castile. Later, in the 15th century, it became part of the dominion of the Constables of Castile, which maintained ownership over the land until the 19th century when the lordships were abolished.

The town centre, after being carefully refurbished, is dotted with manor houses and palaces that were built in the 16th and 17th centuries as a result of the economic boom from trading the wool of Pedraza's large flocks of merino sheep. Wool from Pedraza was exported to northern Europe to make fabric that rivalled the quality and price of the kind made in Flanders.

The main monuments begin at the 11th-century **Puerta de la Villa** (the Town Gate), which was rebuilt

Plaza Mayor

Castle and the Zuloaga Museum

The steep "Calle de las Cuestas"

in the 16th century and once had a jail; it is still the only entrance into town. The 13th-century **castle**, with its imposing tower keep, was where the two sons of Francis I of France were held in captivity, who were handed over by their father as hostages to Charles I of Spain until the accords of the Treaty of Madrid (1526) were complied with, signed after the French monarch's defeat at Pavia. The **Plaza Mayor**, with its porticoes and a splendid line of connected balconies, is considered a superb example of popular Castilian architecture. The initially Romanesque **Church of St. John the Baptist** was eventually reconverted to the Baroque style.

ALBARRACÍN

The Arabs called it Aben Razin, the name of a Berber family, although some authors disagree, pointing to the Celt word alb for "mountain", and ragin, for "vine" or "grape".

Albarracín, whose municipality is one of the largest in the province of Teruel, has a very well preserved town centre that clings to the sides of a mountain rounded by the Guadalaviar River. Its steep narrow streets,

Building façades

whose traditionally-built houses have typical hand-forged ironwork fitted over their windows, bring the visitor straight back to medieval times. Unfortunately, the Spanish Civil War brought with it serious damage, as the town was hotly contested between the Republic's forces and General Franco's rebel troops.

The Albarracín area has been inhabited since prehistoric times, proven by the rock paintings discovered in the Rodeno pine groves. Much later, the Romans built a village over the remains of a Celtic fort, known as St. Mary of the East after it had been Christianised. The Moorish invasion brought the family of Aben Racín to the village. After the break-up of the Cordoba Caliphate, the town of Albarracín became an independent *taifa* kingdom which saw the rule of three kings and lasted over a century. With the arrival of the Almoravids, the area fell within the dominion of the Kingdom of Valencia. In 1285 the town was conquered by Peter III of Aragon, and its strategic position led to the building of the impressive walls that still stand today. In the 16th century, when the walls were no longer needed thanks to the political stability in the region, a quarter grew up outside the *Portal de Molina* (the Mill Gate) and part of the residents, who made their living from agriculture, moved out onto the plain. In the 19th century, after the Peninsular War, Albarracín began its decline which would only worsen after the Civil War.

The town is divided into two areas: the old town with its ***casas colgadas*** (hanging houses) high above the bend in the river, and the Arrabal, which extends

View of Albarracín and its walls

Plaza Mayor

beyond the flood plain of the Guadalaviar. A small trail leads up to its 9th-century **castle**, the old Moorish fort which was used as the residence of the Aben Racín and had its heyday in the 9th century during the time of the *taifa* kingdom of Albarracín. The **walls** (14th century) were built by Christians and are still guarded by two towers, **Engarrada** and **Andador**. The single nave and side chapels of the **Cathedral of El Salvador** (16th century) were built over the remains of a 12th-century Romanesque church. The **Episcopal Palace**, residence of the influential bishops of Albarracín, has a Baroque portal, while the 16th-century Renaissance-style **Casa Consistorial**, the Town Hall, has fine wooden balconies.

BERMEO

In the county of Busturialdea, Bermeo is a great starting point for visiting the Urdaibai Biosphere Reserve, an enormously important ecological area formed by the Oka River estuary.

The rise of its fishing port meant Bermeo would become the largest town in the Lordship of Biscay, which is why it had certain privileges and greater political power than the rest of the towns in the *Juntas*

The Aita Guria Whaling Ship

Hermitage of St. John of Gaztelugatxe

The Port

Generales (representative assemblies) of Biscay. In addition, the kings who visited the Lordship would have to swear their loyalty to the *fueros* or local laws in St. Euphemia's Church in Bermeo.

The first documents that mention Bermeo date back to the 11th century. For example, there is evidence that in 1053 Eneko López and his wife Toda granted the land of Gaztelugatxe to the Monastery of St. John of the Cliff. Today, as in centuries past, the main economy of Bermeo is based on fishing and canning, although tourism has been making more and more inroads as the second local industry, led by the opening of restaurants, bars and rural lodgings.

Among Bermeo's more interesting tourist attractions is the **Hermitage of St. John of Gaztelugatxe** (10th century). Built upon an islet (on the Bermeo-Bakio road) and joined to the mainland by a double-arched bridge, the hermitage can only be accessed by climbing up 231 steps. The **Ercilla Tower** (15th century), high above the port, is home to the **Bermeo Fishermen Museum**, which takes visitors through the history of this seaside town by way of its fishing industry. **St. John's Gate** is the only architectural feature that has survived from the old walled medieval village.

SOS DEL REY CATÓLICO

The location of Sos, perched atop a high outcrop, has long made the town an impenetrable fortress.

The town, brought within the Kingdom of Aragon by Ramiro I in 1044, received a visit from Queen Juana Enríquez (1452) in the midst of the Navarrese Civil War, and as chance would have it, Sos would see the birth of Prince Ferdinand, the future Ferdinand II of Aragon, better known as the Catholic King. This explains why Sos added the words "*Rey Católico*" (Catholic King) to its name.

The finely preserved town centre of Sos led to the government declaring it a Historic-Artistic and Cultural Heritage Site (1968). A stroll through its medieval streets leads to the **Palace of Los Sada** (15th century), built of great stone blocks and the place where Queen Juana gave birth to Prince Ferdinand. Currently it is home to the Ferdinand II of Aragon Interpretation Centre. The **castle** (12th century) was

View of the town

Tower keep of the castle

a strategic point for centuries in the defence of the Navarre-Aragon border. The **medieval exchange**, now a public library, was once the market. The medieval **Jewish quarter**, now called **Barrio Alto**, was formed by some thirty houses. **St. Stephen's Church**, located next to the castle, is composed of the church itself, a crypt and a cloister. Lastly there are the old **gates** of the **town walls**, seven of which are still standing (the gates of Zaragoza, the Queen, Sangüesa, Jaca, Uncastillo, Levant and El Mudo), which bear witness to the fortification of the town. Two kilometres from Sos is the **Monastery of Our Lady of Valentuñana** (17th century), built by the Discalced Carmelites and whose church has a noteworthy Baroque altarpiece (17th century).

Hermitage of St. Lucy

Fideuà

GASTRONOMY

COCIDO MADRILEÑO

This dish, which was originally a favourite among the lower classes, became so popular and renowned that it was included in many of Madrid's best restaurants.

The origins of *cocido madrileño* are similar to those of other Spanish stew dishes (*cocido montañés, cocido alpujarreño, cocido maragato, escudella catalana*, etc.) and some authors claim that it is an evolution of Arabic couscous. Others relate it to *olla podrida* and even with Jewish *adafina*.

Cocido madrileño (Madrid stew) is the most representative dish of the Spanish capital's cuisine. It is popular in the winter and is divided into two or three dishes: first the soup with fine noodles, made with stock, followed by the vegetables, potatoes and chickpeas and, finally, the meat (the last two dishes are usually combined in one in restaurants).

Although now considered to be a typical dish of Madrid, most historians believe that it evolved from the *olla podrida manchega* stew that is mentioned on many occasions in the gastronomic literature of the Golden Age. However, by the end of the 17th century, this dish was already known as belonging to Madrid. Later, at the end of the 19th and beginning of the 20th centuries, *cocido madrileño* was gradually used as a dish in the court and by the wealthy, it became popular and restaurants included it on their menus.

The traditional *cocido madrileño* recipe includes chickpeas, pork shin, chicken, chorizo, carrots, ham end and a ham bone, fatty bacon, onion black pudding, cabbage, garlic and potatoes. The pork shin, the fatty bacon, the ham end and the ham bone are placed in a pan full of water. It is brought to the boil and the foam is removed. The chickpeas, after being in water overnight, are tied in a net, placed in the pan of boiling water and everything is left to cook for two to three hours. The cabbage (chopped), chorizo and black pudding are placed in another pan with some of the stock from the first pan. The garlic is fried in a frying pan and then added to the cabbage when it is cooked. The chickpeas are served on one plate with the boiled meat and vegetables. The thin noodle soup made with the stock is served first.

Cocido madrileño

FABADA ASTURIANA

According to expert gastronomists, fabada is a highlight of the abundant rich cuisine of Asturias, and always tastes better the day after.

Fabada asturiana, or the traditional stew of Asturias, is made with butter beans (*fabes* in Asturian dialect), chorizo, onion black pudding and fatty bacon. It is preferably eaten in winter, as it a high-calorie dish, served hot on two plates: first the beans and then what is known as the *compango*, the chorizo, black pudding and fatty bacon.

Butter beans have been eaten since the 16th century, and *fabada* has formed part of country fare in Asturias since the 18th or 19th centuries. It is strange, however, to find that in *La Regenta*, a novel by Leopoldo Alas "Clarín" that was published in two volumes between 1884 and 1885 and mentions most of the region's customs, there is no mention of *fabada*. According to other authors, *fabada* dates from the 13th and 14th centuries, derived from the *cassoulet* of Languedoc, which was brought into Spain via the Way of St. James.

The first reference to *fabada*, however, is found in a copy of the *El Comercio* newspaper published in Gijón in 1884. So it could well be that *fabada* originated in the 19th or 20th centuries due to the need for high-calorie dishes to help farmers and country folk to withstand the cold, wet winters in the mountains of Asturias.

The best butter beans for making *fabada* are *fabes* from Asturias, protected by a Protected Geographical Indication. They are dry beans (*Phaseolus vulgaris*), of the traditional "Asturian farm" variety, separated from the husk, healthy, whole and clean, sold in the "extra" and "first class" categories.

The beans (*fabes*) have to be cooked for five to eight hours, depending on the variety, on a low heat with the lid half on and half off and occasionally freshening with cold water. While they are cooking, the pan should be shaken every fifteen minutes, but never stirred with a kitchen utensil.

Fabada asturiana

GAZPACHO

Gazpacho is one of the most refreshing dishes in Spanish cuisine and therefore is particularly popular in the summer.

Gazpacho, a cold soup based on olive oil, vinegar and raw vegetables (tomatoes, cucumber, red and green peppers, onion and garlic) is, according to Covarrubias, "food for farm workers and the low classes, who must have named it according to whim…".

Andalusian gazpacho is very famous but its origins, like those of many other dishes, are unknown. Some authors date gazpacho to the Al-Andalus era, albeit in a different version, because the ingredients used now were unknown until the New World was discovered. Modern gazpacho is assumed to be a very old recipe that has constantly evolved. Although tomatoes were brought to Spain from the New World in the 16th century, they were not used in gazpacho until the 19th century, and the same applies to some of its other ingredients.

Gazpacho is a very refreshing soup, traditionally made by washing and finely chopping the tomatoes, cucumber, red and green peppers, onions and garlic, putting them in a bowl and adding a little salt and stale bread previously immersed in oil and vinegar. These ingredients are left in the refrigerator for 24 hours to macerate. Water is then added and the mixture is blended. It is then passed through a sieve and served.

The etymology of the word "gazpacho" is somewhat controversial. According to *Diccionario de lengua española* (2001) it is derived from the Andalusian Arabic *gazpáco*, which in turn comes from the Greek *gazophilakion*, "church collection box", referring to its diversity of content. Sebastián de Covarrubias, in *Tesoro de la lengua castellana o española* (1611), says it comes from "the Tuscan words *guazo* and *guazato*, which mean a liquid stew with some chopped food cooked in it (…); or from the verb *gazaz* which means *succideere*, referring to the pieces into which bread is broken in order to soak better". Finally, Joan Corominas, in *Diccionario crítico-etimológico castellano e hispano* (1954), attributes its origin to a Mozarabic word derived from pre-Roman word *caspa* ("waste"), referring to the pieces of bread and vegetables used in gazpacho.

Gazpacho andaluz

MIGAS

Migas*, or shepherds'* migas*, was one of the most typical dishes of the migratory shepherds in the Middle Ages.*

This dish makes use of leftover stale bread, although it is also made with flour in south-eastern Spain. The origin of *migas* (literally "crumbs") is found in Moroccan couscous, which started to be made in Christendom with bread, adding some fried fatty bacon to distinguish it from other Muslim or Jewish dishes in which bacon was forbidden. Shepherds, as they watched over their flocks at night in winter time, needed high-calorie meals and *migas* is perfect for keeping out the cold. It was also considered to be a complete meal, as it contained proteins, carbohydrates and fats.

Migas is eaten in many Spanish regions, including La Mancha, La Alcarria, Murcia, Campo de Cartagena, Andalusia, Extremadura, Castile and León and Aragon, and it generally consists of frying chopped stale bread, previously dampened with water, with garlic and a little olive oil until it takes on a golden colour.

The dish can be eaten with a large variety of both sweet (grapes, pomegranates, etc.) and savoury (fried bacon, fried eggs, peppers, chorizo, etc.) foodstuffs. In some regions, *migas* is cooked with paprika, which makes it red. *Migas* is usually served in the same pan that it is cooked in, and everyone dips in with a spoon.

There are many varieties of *migas*, including "*migas ruleras*" (because when cooked they are able to "roll" down a slope), typical of La Mancha, "*migas aragonesas*" (served with grapes), "*migas andaluzas*" (adding anise), "*gachasmigas*" (made with flour), typical of the Campo de Cartagena and Murcia, "*migas de Almería*" (made with semolina, like couscous) and "*migas extremeñas*" (usually served with sardines).

***Migas* tapa**

Migas

PAELLA

Paella from Valencia has evolved and paellas of all kinds are currently available which can satisfy even the most demanding of palates.

Paella, the traditional dish of Valencia and possibly the most international of Spanish cuisine, has its origins in La Albufera (Valencia), when the Arabs brought rice to the Peninsula (8th century). Rice growing quickly spread along the Valencia coast and it was soon part of the peasants' diet. Also, the pan from which this dish takes its name, the paella (*patella* in Latin), was used as early as during the Roman colonisation of Hispania. Some authors therefore maintain that it is an Italian word that came to Spain from Naples when that kingdom belonged to the Spanish crown.

Originally the paella of Valencia was a meal for poor people (eel fishers from La Albufera and farm workers), but it became a classic Spanish dish over time. As paella became increasingly popular, both in Spain and abroad, its original composition, based on rice, chicken, duck, rabbit and snails, evolved to a large variety of recipes (seafood paella, mixed paella, vegetable paella, etc.). The multiple versions of paella are now served all over Spain.

To protect the original paella recipe, the Regional Ministry of Agriculture (Regional Government of Valencia), in collaboration with the Regulatory Council of the "Rice from Valencia" designation of origin, has published a list of the ingredients that must form part of any paella sold under the name of "paella from Valencia". These ingredients, traditionally used in the Valencia region, are chicken, rabbit, green beans (*ferraura*), a type of butter bean (*garrafó*), tomatoes, rice, olive oil, water, saffron and salt. Depending on the region, garlic, artichoke, duck, paprika, snails and rosemary are also admitted.

Paella with eggs, prawns and peppers

Paella

SPANISH OMELETTE

The potato omelette, also known as Spanish omelette, is one of the most international dishes in our cuisine.

The origins of the potato omelette are unknown but they are linked to when the potato (*Solanum tuberosum*), a tuber from America, was brought to Spain. Apparently, the potato omelette originated in Villanueva de la Serena (Badajoz) and is supposed to have been invented by José de Tena Godoy y Malfeito, the Marquis of Robledo, while he was looking for food to mitigate a famine at the end of the 18th century.

Only eggs and potatoes are required for an omelette, although some cooks add onion to make them juicier. The potatoes are washed and peeled and sliced into medium-sized fine slices. They are fried in olive oil, starting on a high flame (the onion is fried with the potatoes) for a few minutes and then turning the heat down. They are stirred occasionally to prevent them from sticking to the pan and burning. They are ready in ten to fifteen minutes.

The potatoes are taken from the pan, drained of oil and placed in a large bowl. The eggs are beaten in a bowl, salt is added and they are put to one side. A few drops of oil are added to the frying pan and the potato and egg mixture is added; when done on one side, the omelette is turned over with the help of a plate.

The first document containing a clear reference to a potato omelette comes from Navarre. A note sent by an anonymous peasant to the Assembly of Navarre in 1817 describes the terrible living conditions of local peasants and, as part of a list of the few foodstuffs consumed by mountain dwellers, it mentions "...two or three eggs in an omelette for five or six [people], because our women know how to make them large and thick, with a few eggs and mixing potatoes, *atapurres* [from the Basque *otapur*, "crumbs"] of bread or something else".

Courgette omelette

Spanish omelette

CHURROS

Churro *dough, a simple combination of flour, water, sugar and salt, is placed in a "churrera" to obtain its characteristic shape.*

Churros form part of typical Spanish breakfasts and afternoon snacks, either with a cup of coffee, hot chocolate or on their own.

According to several authors, *churros*, a mixture of water, corn flour, yeast and olive oil (and butter in some recipes) come from Muslim cuisine. However, their consumption is documented in Catalonia in the early 19th century. For one group of historians, they originated with the need for shepherds to be able to cook food outdoors that did not need many utensils: a frying pan and a little olive oil, flour and water were sufficient to make a high-calorie meal that protected against the cold. Those who support this theory say that the word "churro" comes from "churra" (a breed of sheep that originated in Castile y León, the oldest in Spain), maintaining that the long, twisted shape of the *churro* is like the horns of those sheep.

Nearly all over Spain, the word "churro" refers to a long, round kind of fritter, which is referred to as "fruit of the pan" in the *Diccionario* of the Royal Academy of Language. In Granada, they are known as "jeringos", a reference to the syringe-shaped utensil used to make them.

The difference between a "churro" and a "porra" lies in the dough. *Churro* dough is made with very hot water, to scald the yeast, while *porra* dough is made with warm water, so that the yeast ferments and creates a characteristic spongy texture.

From Spain, *churros* spread to Latin America, where they are also popular, and in the last few years they have been found in American cuisine after their success in Tokyo, Osaka and Shanghai thanks to chains such as Xooro and Le Churro.

Churros and *porras*

ROSCÓN DE REYES

The Roscón de Reyes*, an example of Roman pastries, was adapted to the Catholic religious ritual after the Christianisation of the Roman Empire.*

On 6th January it is traditionally eaten for breakfast or tea. It is decorated with glazed fruit and sugar, and orange blossom water is used to give it its particular flavour. Nowadays, they are usually filled with cream, truffle or custard.

Roscón de Reyes, a typical pastry that is eaten in Spain at Epiphany, 6th January, is of pagan origin. Several authors relate it to the Roman Saturnalia in honour of Saturn, the god of agriculture and civilisation, which are held from 17th December to celebrate the winter solstice and the end of the last crop of the year. This festival involved cooking a kind of torte made from honey and decorated with dates or figs. During these festivities, servants were served by their masters, as they were on an equal footing.

In the 3rd century, a dry bean was added to this circular pastry. Whoever received the bean in his or her portion was considered to be a "king of kings", as beans symbolised fertility. When Hispania became Christian, Saturnalia disappeared and the torte with its bean became the circular pastry now known as a *roscón*. In the 18th century, a pastry cook at the Court of Louis XV in France inserted a gold coin (according to some sources, a medallion of gold and rubies), as well as the bean, after which the bean was bad luck and the coin meant good luck. This custom was brought to Spain by King Philip VI, and over the years the coin was replaced by a clay figure. According to custom, whoever finds the bean has to pay for the *roscón*.

The *Roscón de Reyes* tradition was exported to South America in the 16th century, where it became popular in countries like Mexico, where it is eaten with hot chocolate or *atole*. In Spain, these pastries can be found in cafés a few days before Epiphany for breakfast or an afternoon snack, with a cup of coffee or hot chocolate.

Roscón de Reyes

TORRIJAS

Torrijas, *a pastry associated with Lent and Holy Week, were made to take advantage of stale bread.*

Torrijas consist of slices of bread soaked in milk, or wine and honey, with spices (such as cinnamon). After being soaked in egg, they are fried in very hot oil (they are sprinkled with sugar or coated in liqueur or syrup before serving).

This high-calorie dish was eaten by Catholics who did not eat meat during Lent, to fill their stomachs before a hard day's work. So rich were *torrijas* that they were also given to women after childbirth to help them to recover.

The first reference to *torrijas* dates from the 15th century, in a piece by Juan del Encina (1468-1529), a poet, musician and playwright, who wrote "Honey and a lot of eggs to make *torrijas*". The first recipes, however, are from later dates, in *Libro del arte de cozina* (1607), by Domingo Hernández Maceras, the cook at Colegio Mayor de Oviedo in Salamanca, and in *Arte de cozina, pastelería, vizcochería y conservería* (1611) by Francisco Martínez Motiño, a Golden Age cook and writer who cooked for three kings over more than thirty years: Philip II, Philip III and Philip IV.

Different versions of *torrijas* are also found in France (*pain perdu*), Britain (*French toast*, in reference to *pain perdu*), Germany (*arme ritter*), Switzerland (*Fotzelschnitten*), Hungary (*bundás kenyér*), Portugal (*rabanadas*) and in South American countries such as Colombia, Chile, Ecuador or Peru, where they are known as "French toast" in reference to *pain perdu* or "lost bread".

In the early 20th century, during Lent, *torrijas* were served in many taverns of Madrid with a glass of wine, and they are now often eaten for dessert in Holy Week.

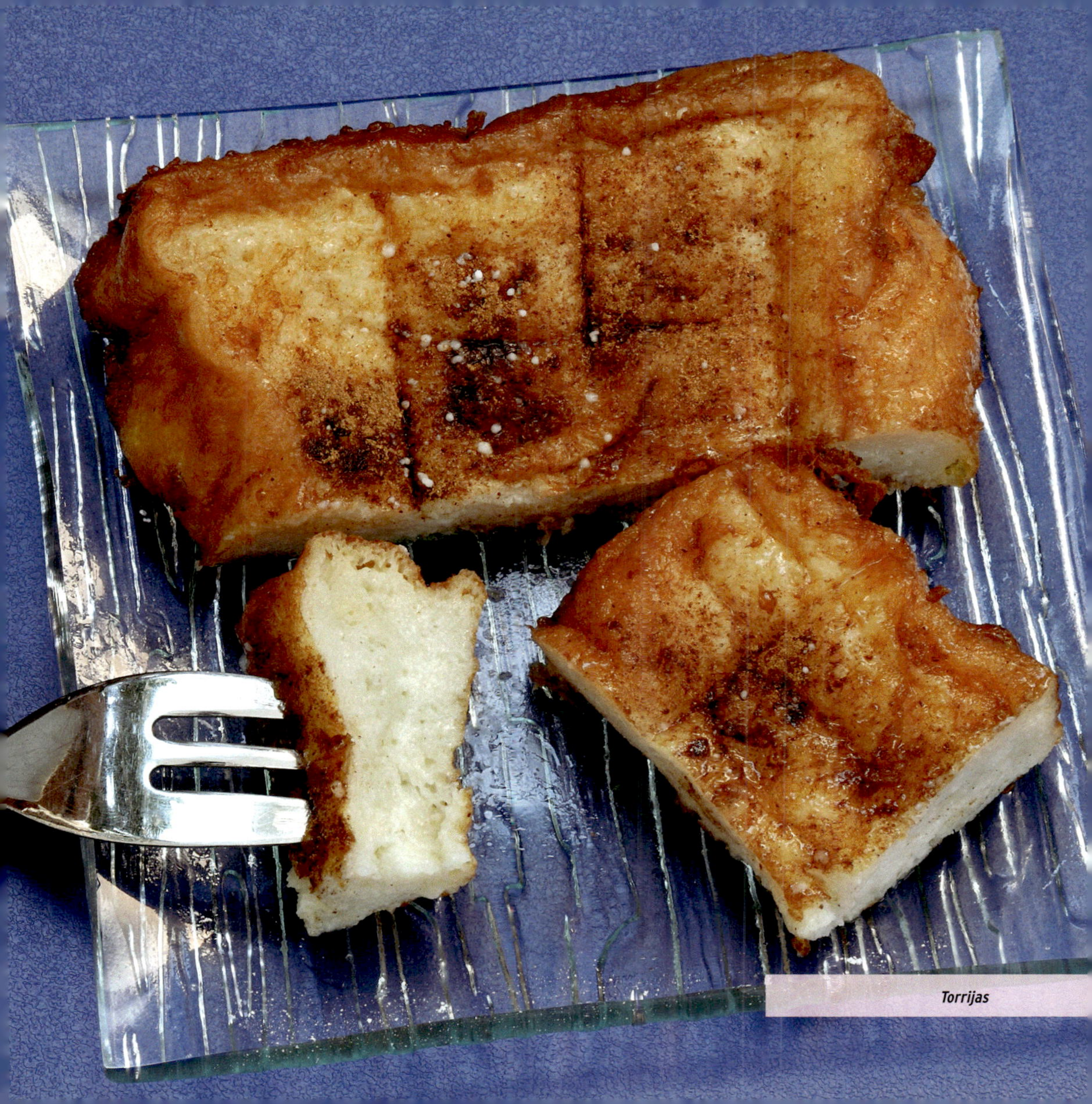

Torrijas

NOUGAT

Christmas in Spain is characterised by eating nougat, a sweet based on almonds and honey that dates back to Arabic times.

Nougat (called *turrón* in Spanish), a sweet obtained after cooking honey and which is sold in the form of bars or tortes (Agramunt nougat), is a typical Christmas dessert in Spain.

There are numerous varieties of nougat sold in Spain, including Xixona nougat (soft), Alicante nougat (hard), Agramunt, Xerta, burned yolk, truffle, chocolate (dark or white, with nuts, rice or almonds), coconut, walnut, marzipan, pineapple, yoghurt, etc. Indeed, there are as many varieties as there are renowned pastry cooks, and nougat producers launch new types every year to satisfy the most demanding of palates.

Historians claim that it originated in Arabia, as shown by *Kitab al-adwiya al-Musfrada* or *Book of simple medicines*, a treatise about the use of simple animal, vegetable or mineral substances, written by Ibn al-Wafid (1008-1074), a botanist and pharmacist from Toledo of Arabic origin whose work includes references to *turun*. The Muslims brought nougat to Spain and other Mediterranean countries. However, the first clear reference to nougat is found in *La generosa paliza* (1570), by Lope de Rueda, when Dalagón says: "You said what? You ate the pound of nougat from Alicante that was on the desk...!" The first recipe, however, is found in an anonymous book, *Manual de mujeres* (16th century). The custom of eating nougat at Christmas was established in Spain by the 16th century, when it was only made in Xixona and Alicante.

Almond paste

Nougat

DESIGNATIONS OF ORIGIN

Designations of Origin are legally granted to food and farm products whose quality and characteristics are directly linked to the geographical area where they are made.

Manufacturers covered by a Designation of Origin are under the obligation to ensure high quality in their products and use traditional production methods to guarantee consumer satisfaction. Each Designation of Origin has a Regulatory Council that is responsible for ensuring that the products sold meet the established standards and for authorising products to carry the regulatory labels and symbols that guarantee their quality.

Paprika from La Vera

Logo

The standards applicable to Designations of Origin have been unified throughout the European Union, fostering the organisation of the production sector and its products' access to national and international markets.

In 1564, Spanish law was already protecting Ribadavia wine: "Ribadavia wine must be from the town of Ribadavia as far as the St. Clodius spring [the original text goes on to list specific places](...) Wine comes to the town from places where it is not good and it is a problem because beneath a cask of good wine

Artichokes from Tudela

the merchants sell wine that is not so good, and the buyers are deceived, and this wine cannot be shipped by sea". According to other authors, there was legislation similar to present day Designations of Origin in the times of the Roman emperor Diocletian (c. 244-311). In the year 301, this emperor issued the *Edictum de pretiis maximis rerum venalium* or *Edict of maximum prices*, to fix the price of around 1,300 products, the cost of their labour and record the region where they were produced to prevent buyers from being deceived and rising inflation.

Dry salted meat from León

In Spain there are a large variety of products covered by Designations of Origin, from wines (Rioja, Priorato, Ribera del Duero, Jerez, Somontano, Ribeiro, Toro, etc.) to cheeses (Cabrales, Los Beyos, Mahón, Manchego, Tupí, Torta del Casar, etc.), and including ham (Guijuelo, Dehesa de Extremadura, Teruel, Jamón de Huelva, Los Pedroches, etc.), cold cuts (Salchichón de Vic, Sobrasada de Mallorca, Botillo del Bierzo, Lacón Gallego, Cecina de León, etc.), vegetables (Alcachofa de Tudela, Chufa de Valencia, Berenjena de Almagro, Ajo Morado de Las Pedroñeras, Espárragos de Navarra, etc.), oil (Lucena, Bajo Aragón, Siurana, Baena, Priego de Córdoba, etc.), vinegar (Condado de Huelva, Jerez, etc.), licueurs (Palo de Mallorca, Orujo de Galicia, Pacharán, Gin de Menorca, etc.), legumes (Judías de El Barco, Judías del Ganxet, Lenteja de la Armuña, etc.), meat (Carne de la Sierra del Guadarrama, Cordero de Navarra, Lechazo de Castilla y León, etc.), pastries (Mazapán de Toledo, Ensaimada de Mallorca, Tarta de Santiago), etc.

SPANISH HAM

Spanish ham, the most international and exclusive Spanish product, is largely produced in the south of the Peninsula, the home of large herds of Iberian pigs.

There are currently four Designations of Origin covering Spanish ham: Dehesa de Extremadura, Los Pedroches, Jamón de Huelva and Guijuelo. The secret behind the excellent quality of these hams lies in the rear legs of the Iberian pigs used to make them, by a traditional system that includes four basic processes: salting, cleaning, settling and drying or maturation. The best pigs for making these hams are Iberian, either 100% or 75% pure; they are fattened in the last few months of their lives when they run free in the countryside, where they feed on acorns, grass and tubers in fields full of holm oaks, cork oaks and gall oaks.

After the animals are slaughtered, the hams are salted. This process takes on average around one day per kilo of fresh meat. The hams are placed in temperature-controlled chambers, with layers of salt between them, so that the salt slowly penetrates the meat. After this process, the salt is rinsed off the surface and the hams are taken to a settling chamber, from where they are transferred to natural drying facilities where they are cured by the currents of air that master ham makers control by simply opening and closing the windows. Finally, at the end of August or the beginning of September, the hams are taken to storage for maturation, for a time that depends on the quality (usually from 5 to 24 months), although this period largely depends on the standards established by the Regulatory Councils of the different Designations of Origin. During this final process, the hams are coated with different fungi to promote maturation and provide their particular, unique flavour. At the same time, there are a series of enzyme and metabolic reactions that define the hams' final sensory properties.

Spanish hams have been deservedly renowned since the Roman colonisation, when they were exported to Rome and served to emperors. At that time the best hams were made by the Ceretani, an Iberian people in the Pyrenees.

Acorn-fed cured ham from Huelva

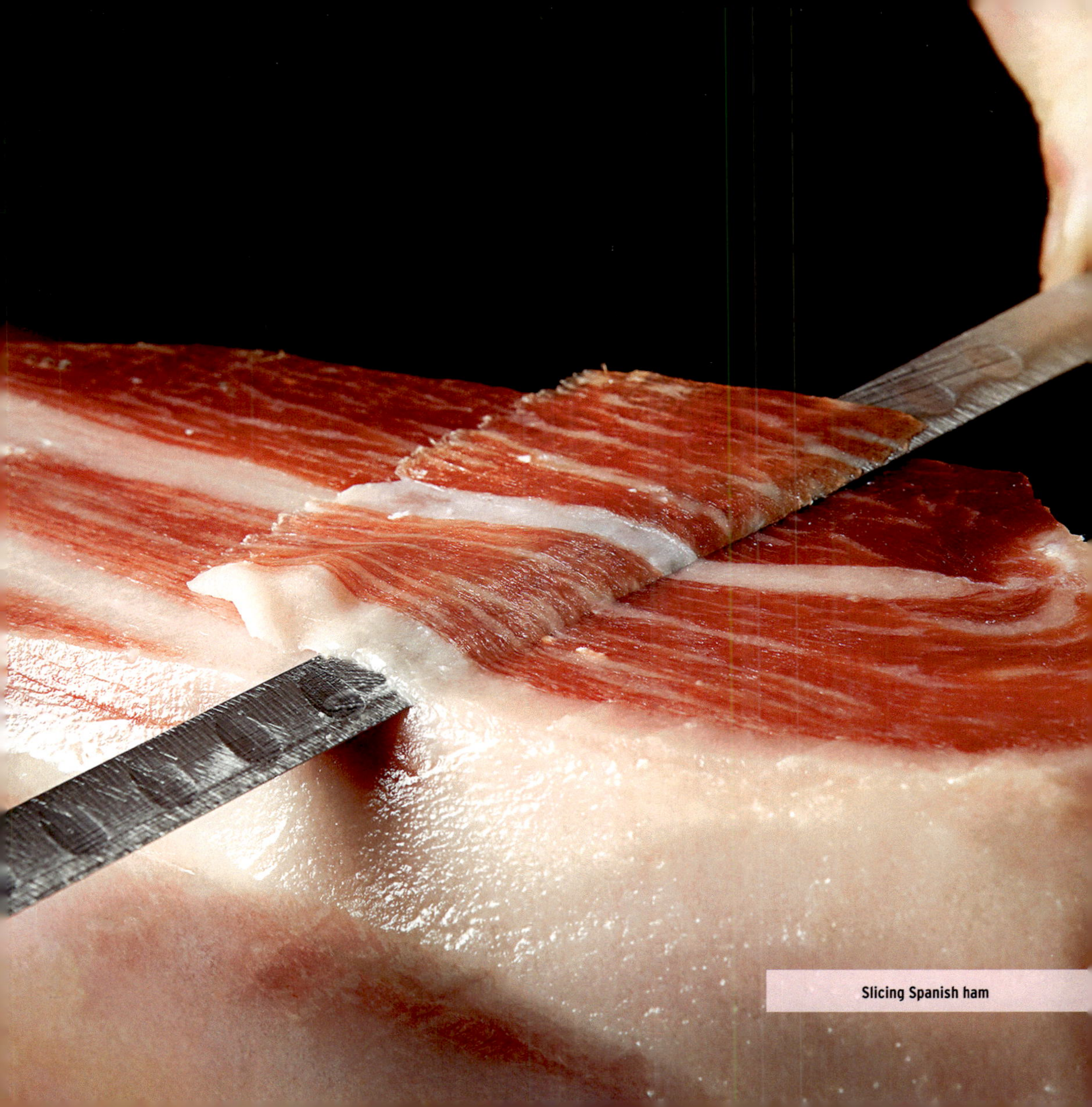

Slicing Spanish ham

OLIVE OIL

According to many experts, Spanish olive oil is the best in the world, and is crucial in what is now known as the "Mediterranean diet".

The inhabitants of the Peninsula have used oil since ancient times, thanks to the many olive trees growing in the Mediterranean climate, to replace animal fat. The best olive groves are currently found in the Mediterranean basin. In Spain, they are primarily grown in Andalusia, Extremadura, Castile, Catalonia, Valencia, Murcia and Aragon.

Bottle of extra virgin oil

The oil-making process currently comprises six phases: olive washing, milling, pressing, separation of the oil from "alpechin" (fetid vegetable water produced by olives when pressed with boiling water to obtain oil), ageing and storage. The olives are washed with special machines, although this process used to be by hand, and the pit was removed under the mistaken idea that it altered the properties of the resulting oil. The olives then go to the mill and when they have been reduced to a paste, they are stored in straw baskets and piled on top of each other for pressing. The first oil, extracted at low pressure, is of excellent quality and is called "extra virgin oil". In Spain there are more than thirty Designations of Origin for oil, which correspond to the most important manufacturing regions. Extra virgin oil, the best quality of all, has very specific sensory properties and each type of oil is different, depending on the region of production. However, in general the flavour depends on the variety of olive used to obtain the oil. The colour comes from the mixture of chlorophyll and carotenoid pigments. Oil also contained oleins (72 percent), stearin and palmitin.

Olives

To prevent it from turning rancid, olive oil must be stored in full bottles (with the least possible

Olive grove

Tapa of toast with oil and brie cheese

air), tightly closed and in a cool, dark place (from 10-15°C). When cooking, if oil is heated to more than 120°C it loses its characteristic colour, which it recovers as it cools. However, if it is heated to an extremely high temperature it is spoilt.

ANCHOVIES

Anchovies eaten in Spain are largely preserved although they are also ingredients in some sauces and salads.

Anchovies cured in brine are very popular in Spanish cuisine on account of their wonderful flavour. Two types of anchovy are fished for human consumption, and the *Engraulidae* genre is the most plentiful in the Cantabrian and Mediterranean seas. However, excessive fishing in the last twenty years has drastically reduced the catch and several fishing moratoriums have been necessary in the Cantabrian Sea to guarantee the species' continuity.

The towns that are currently the most famous for their salted anchovies are Santoña (Cantabria) and L'Escala (Girona). It was in Santoña where they first started to cut anchovies into fillets, as they are usually presented now. They first clean the fish, without

Port of L'Escala

Tasting anchovies

Preparing anchovy fillets in L'Escala

rinsing, and then place them in a container between layers of sea salt for storing in a cool place. A fortnight later the container is opened and any water is drained off The anchovies are left in salt for four to five months, after which they are ready to eat. The salt is removed, they are left in water for around six hours, the bones are removed, they are rinsed again, left to drain or dried with kitchen towel and served with a little extra virgin olive oil.

WINE AND CAVA

Spanish wine and cava are world renowned, thanks to their production methods and the good quality of their grapes.

Spanish wine was deservedly renowned during the Roman colonisation. Wines, packed in amphorae, from Gallaecia, Beticae and Tarraconensis were transported in merchant ships to the far corners of the Roman empire. Authors such as Pliny the Elder and Martial mentioned wine from Hispania in their writings, praising its many qualities. Even during the Arabic period (8th to 15th century), and contrary to what you might think, wine was sold as normal and some Muslim doctors even prescribed it as medicine. After the reconquest, Spanish wine was again exported, especially to England. However, the real boom in Spanish wine came in the 19th century, when French vineyards were destroyed by a plague of phylloxera. The loss of the French vineyards boosted the sale of

Codorniu winery in Sant Sadurni d'Anoia

Ysios winery in Laguardia

Wine and cava

Spanish wine on the international markets, especially Rioja. Winemakers, particularly in Haro, decided to invest heavily in modernising their production, and they hired French oenologists to teach them the techniques that had given French wines their high quality and prestige. At the same time, several French winemakers moved to La Rioja and introduced the crop and harvesting techniques that they used in France along with ageing the wines in cellars in oak casks Phylloxera also affected and devastated Spanish vineyards at the end of the 19th century. The implantation of phylloxera-resistant American stocks led to the recovery of the Spanish wine sector.

Furthermore, cava (champagne that for legal reasons is marketed under that name) started to be produced in the 19th century in the Penedès area between the provinces of Barcelona and Tarragona. Cava can be defined as a sparkling white wine made in the same way as champagne (*méthode champenoise*). Cava is made from wine using the traditional procedure and is then drawn from the barrel to be bottled. In this phase, sugar and yeast are added to the wine. When it ferments, they produce the carbon dioxide (bubbles) that are typical of cava and its characteristic aroma. Bottles of cava rest horizontally in the dark at a temperature of around 15°C for nine months. They are then placed upside down in "pupitres" or racks and turned one eighth of a circle every day so that the traces of yeast reach the neck of the bottle and can be removed by disgorging (the bottle is opened and part of the liquid is allowed to drain out). The lost liquid is replaced by what is called "expedition liqueur" (sugar dissolved in white wine or liquor) which, depending on the amount of sugar it contains, determines the type of cava (only wine is added to brut nature and extra brut).

González Byass winery in Jerez de la Frontera

Pedro Domecq winery in Jerez de la Frontera

SANGRIA

Sangria, an alcoholic beverage made from wine, is one of the most typical drinks in the summer at mealtimes. It apparently originated towards the end of the 18th century somewhere in South America, possibly the Antilles, and it was brought to Spain in the mid-19th century. Father Esteban Torres, in his *Diccionario del castellano*, says: "[Sangria is a] drink invented by the English that is popular in the English and French colonies of America". This appears to be confirmed by the English word *sangaree* which comes from the Spanish "sangría", in turn derived from the Latin *sanguis, sanguinis*, "blood", due to its colour. Sangria came to be known as "wine lemonade" in some Spanish colonies. Sangria is currently protected by a Protected Geographical Indication, and its production as a PGI is limited to sangria made in Spain and Portugal.

Jar of sangria

Sangria is prepared with red wine, preferably young and slightly fruity, sugar to taste, a little lemon juice, orange juice and fresh fruit cut into small pieces (peach, apricot, pear, apple, banana, strawberry, etc.). Some people like to add a cinnamon stick. The mixture is left to macerate for two or three hours, and some people add a sparkling orange or lemon beverage before serving. It is served in a transparent glass jar.

Zurracapote or *zurra* is made in some parts of Castile y León; it is like sangria but left to macerate for several days to increase its alcohol content, as the sugar is converted into alcohol.

ORUJO

This "aguardiente" or liqueur, made in many Spanish regions, is extremely popular in Galicia, where it is classified as the region's most traditional beverage.

Orujo, a drink made from grape skins, is produced in several Spanish regions, especially in Cantabria, Galicia and the province of León. *Orujo*, derived from the Latin *involucrum*, which means "wrapping", originated in Cantabria, in the Liébana valley, where the records of some monasteries show that it was produced in the 16th century. In that period, *orujo* and wine were used as currency, and also to pay taxes in many areas. Until the last quarter of the 20th century, when laws were passed about drinks bottled for sale after hundreds died from using toxic cooking oil in 1981, *orujo* was only made privately. In Galicia, for instance, *alambiqueiros* were very popular. They would travel the country with their copper stills or *alambiques* to distil the grape skins that families kept after pressing the grapes to make wine. The new laws forced bottled drinks to pay marketing taxes and all the small producers disappeared, giving way to large companies. However, families in Galicia, Cantabria and León continue to make homemade *orujo* for their own consumption (its sale is forbidden).

Aguardientes from Galicia

***Orujo* from Galicia**

Orujo is distilled from the grape skins that are left over after grapes are pressed to make wine. They

Grape skins and stills

are pressed to obtain a weak wine which is taken to the still to make *orujo*. Spanish law classifies *orujo* as a by-product of grapes. For the last 25 years, Galicia has had the "Orujo de Galicia" Geographical Indication, which covers "aguardiente de bagazo" and aged "aguardiente de bagazo", together with herb "aguardiente" and coffee and herb liqueurs made with grape skins from Galician vineyards. The systems used to control the production processes in this PGI are traditional distillation by still or heating by steam, which obtains a high quality product.

CIDER

Cider, the most traditional beverage in some northern Spanish regions, is obtained by fermenting apple juice.

Cider is a low alcohol content beverage (around 3%) made from fermented apple juice. The word "cider" comes from the Latin *sicera*, which in turn comes from the Hebrew *shekar*, "drink that intoxicates". The origins of cider are found in Egypt and Byzantium, in the years before Christianity. For Atlantic peoples, cider was a nectar of the gods and heroes and, according to Celtic tradition, it came from the island of Avalon (the island of apples). However, the first document that refers to cider as such is the *Capitulare de Villis*, a legislative document from the 9th century, which was drafted to organise trade at the time of Charlemagne. In the early 20th century, cider was defined as "a drink with an amber-like colour, healthy, tonic, hygienic, refreshing, with a sweet and sour flavour and a very pleasant aroma". It was also considered to have therapeutic properties, especially for diabetics, due to the polyphenols contained in apples

Cider from Asturias

Pouring cider

which help to regulate blood sugar and stimulate the pancreas to secrete insulin.

Cider, a traditional beverage in many countries, is made by pressing or crushing apples to obtain their juice. The juice or must is left to ferment and at the end of the process it is decanted to separate the sediments and then bottled. In Spain, cider is primarily consumed in Asturias, the Basque Country and Cantabria, at meal times or accompanied by snacks.

Cider drinking has always been a social occasion and it is always poured from a height so that it comes into contact with the edge of the glass, leading to oxygenation. In Asturias, by tradition everyone drinks cider from the same glass.

Viking Festival in Catoira, Pontevedra

TRADITIONAL FESTIVALS

BANDO DE LA HUERTA

The Bando de la Huerta *parade in Murcia is held on Easter Tuesday as part of the festivities marking the onset of spring and the first crops.*

This festival is a tribute to the popular traditions of the inhabitants of the fertile land of Murcia (*huertanos*). The locals wear typical costumes, reminiscent of both the Moorish style and the Spanish court in the 16th century. The women's costumes include underskirts (in the cold parts of Murcia, women used to wear flannel underskirts), and the men's involve wide trousers. Due to the variety and quality of the embroidery on the costumes of both men and women, they can be considered to be veritable works of art. However, they are mainly known for the large number of embellishments they bear. This type of costume became established in the 17th century as a way of reaffirming Murcia's identity versus the new fashions arising in the French court of Louis XIV. Towards the mid-19th century, the Industrial Revolution led to a decline in traditional clothing and it

Typical costumes

Procession of the Virgin of Fuensanta

gradually became used only during popular holidays and festivals.

The origins of this event date back to the Murcia carnival in 1851, when some young local lads from the merchant classes decided to organise a parade to make fun of the *huertanos*. This idea did not take root and, indeed, disappeared for ten years. However, it was recovered from 1876 to 1879, when the local merchants allowed the *huertanos* to take the opportunity to make fun of their own customs. Because of flooding that did a lot of damage, the festival was cancelled in 1879 and did not take place again until 1900. Nowadays, the celebrations commence with a Mass known as "Misa Huertana", which is held in front of the cathedral's Baroque door. This is followed by a procession with the image of the Virgin of Fuensanta, the city's patron saint. The "Bando de la Huerta" parade takes place in the afternoon, with floats loaded with typical products grown in the fertile land of Murcia. At the same time, squares and gardens fill with stalls loaded with traditional local dishes.

BATTLE OF WINE

In the town of Haro, in Rioja, the Battle of Wine takes place on St Peter's Day, with numerous pilgrims celebrating the Felices de Bilibio festival.

During the Battle of Wine (29th June), the participants throw red wine over each other until their clothes are all a purple colour. The battle is held on

Battle of Wine in Haro

Pilgrimage to the ridges of Bilibio

the ridges of Bilibio, around 6 km from Haro; this was the home of Felices de Bilibio, a hermit (6th century) who was the Master of St. Emilian for three years before he retired to the Distertian or Cogollan hills. Felices de Bilibio died in 520 and was buried on the mountain where he lived. In 1090, his remains were carried by Abbot Blas, accompanied by twelve friars, to Yuso Monastery, after obtaining the authorisation of King Alfonso VI the Brave of León (1047-1109), the son of Ferdinand I and his wife, Queen Sancha of León.

In the 18th century, a chapel was built on the ridges of Bilibio to which the people of Haro went in pilgrimage. This was the origin of today's Battle of Wine, because after mass the pilgrims would eat, drink plenty of wine and organise a few brawls, throwing wine over each other to stain their clothes. This is

Battle of Wine in Haro

how the Battle of Wine began, although it was initially criticised by some pilgrims, especially the women who were not pleased to have their dresses stained.

By 1949, the custom of throwing wine was firmly rooted among the participants in the Bilibio pilgrimage. The festival gradually gained in popularity and it is now the main part of the pilgrimage which attracts people from all over Spain, wearing T-shirts to participate in this singular, and harmless, battle. The pilgrimage is led by the "Regidor Síndico" (trustee alderman) on horseback. When he reaches the ridges of Bilibio, he dismounts and places the Haro banner on the top of the mountain. This is followed by Mass, and then the battle. Some people continue to criticise the event, however, as they feel that the Battle of Wine is a way of making a religious event pagan.

CARNIVAL

The Santa Cruz de Tenerife Carnival, the most important held in Spain, attracts thousands of Spanish and international visitors every year.

A carnival started to be held in Tenerife in the mid-16th century. It was famous by the 18th century, and in the 19th *tapaderas* started to appear; they were high society ladies who mixed with the populace during the carnival wearing masks. In 1925 Santa Cruz de Tenerife Town Hall drew up the first carnival programme. Little by little, the Tenerife carnival took on its current composition, with the participation of *rondallas* (bands of street musicians), *comparsas* (groups of people wearing the same costumes), *murgas* (smaller groups of musicians), etc. The 1936-1939 Civil War put an end to the carnival, as it was prohibited by Franco. Nevertheless, it continued in a clandestine fashion. It was recovered in all its current glory after 1976, when democracy returned to Spain.

There are two very different parts to the Tenerife carnival: the official programme and the people in the streets. In the former there are around a hundred

Queen of the Tenerife Carnival

A *murga* parading during the Tenerife carnival

Make-up is an important part of the carnival

groups (*murgas*, *comparsas*, groups dressed up, etc.) while the latter is taken over by local people and tourists alike who take the party to the streets. The Carnival Queen is elected during a great gala the Wednesday before carnival weekend. The candidates are paraded during the gala, wearing rich costumes that can weigh from 150 to 200 kilos; they actually move on small wheels. A jury, made up of councillors and celebrities, votes and elects the queen, and the sceptre of honour is handed over to her by the mayor. Some of the costumes in this contest can cost as much as €20,000.

CASTELLERS

Castells *("castles"), human towers made up of people called* castellers, *have been declared Cultural Heritage by UNESCO.*

Castells and *castellers* are derived from the "Valencian dances" held during religious processions. At the end of each procession, the participants would build a

A *castell* with one person per layer

The *pinya*, or base of a *castell*

figure rising a few feet above the ground and, over time, this tradition became independent and acquired its own identity. By the 17th century, the custom of creating *castells* had spread through southern Catalonia, and in 1770 there is documentary evidence of a *castell* built in l'Arboç (Tarragona). By 1790, the word *castell* was commonly used to refer to these human towers and distinguish them from "Valencian dances". The first *colles castelleres* or groups that build *castells* were established in Valls (Tarragona) in the 19th century. Finally, in the 1980s the *colles castelleres* recovered their popularity in Catalonia and *castells* are now always part of the region's most important festivals.

Building a *castell* is a difficult technique that is only learned with years of practice. The base of the *castell*,

***Castell* in front of Barcelona City Hall**

the *pinya*, is formed by a large group of *castellers* whose role is to balance and support the *castell*. The *tronc*, the visible part of the *castell*, determines its degree of difficulty, according to the number of people involved. The *pom de dalt*, the name given to the top three layers of the *castell*, is crowned by the figure of the *enxaneta*, as the child at the top of the *castell* is called. Despite the difficulties and risks involved in *castells*, there have only ever been four fatal accidents.

The clothes worn by *castellers* consist of a coloured long-sleeved shirt with an embroidered coat of arms of their *colla*, white trousers made out of strong material to withstand the traction of the *castellers* as they climb to the top of the tower, a long black cummerbund, which acts as protection for the back and supports the *castellers* as they climb, plus a red triangular scarf with white polka dots. Originally the scarf was worn on the head to protect the hair from the feet of the *castellers* who climbed to the top of the *castell*. In some *colles* the *castellers* tie their scarves to their knees to provide something for their colleagues to hold onto. This uniform was first used by the Vella dels Xiquets *colla* from Valls in the Barcelona World's Fair in 1929, and it soon took root among other groups.

CHIRIGOTAS

Chirigotas, *the most important artistic aspect of the Cadiz carnival, are part of its international renown.*

At the end of the 16th century, historian Agustín de Horozco left the first documentary references to the Cadiz carnival. In the 18th century, the crown prohibited masked balls in an attempt to do away with the carnival, but these laws were never respected and the Cadiz carnival continued to be held privately. There was another attempt to ban it in the 19th century, but as on the previous occasions it was not successful. In 1862 Cadiz City Hall organised the first carnival programme, in an attempt to limit participation in the streets and attract visitors to the city. In 1884 the carnival and its *chirigotas* were held with some restrictions and a municipal ordinance established that the words to songs first had to be submitted to the censor. In 1937, during the Civil War, the Cadiz carnival was again prohibited, but it returned in full force in 1948. At that time, as Franco and his government censured all public events in an attempt to limit freedom of speech, especially when opinions were expressed against the established

Cadiz carnival

***Chirigota* contest in the Gran Teatro Falla**

order, the lyrics of the songs were not particularly scathing and indeed they were nothing compared to the songs of today, which primarily criticise politicians. The *chirigotas* that are sung during the Cadiz carnival nowadays are very funny and satirical. *Chirigotas* are short songs, with very simple music and words, which contain scathing criticism of people involved in politics, high society or sport. During the Cadiz carnival, no one is exempt from being mentioned in a *chirigota*. The Gran Teatro Falla, in Cadiz, is the site of a contest during the carnival, in which all the important groups participate. Each *chirigota*, or carnival group, comprises from seven to twelve people who sing a repertoire written by themselves accompanied by drums, guitars, kazoos, mandolins, lutes and *güiros* (percussion instruments made from gourds). The members of the *chirigota* have to wear costumes related to the subject of their songs. *Chirigotas* have become so popular in recent times that they are broadcast live on television and their audience grows every year.

DESCENT OF THE RIVER SELLA

The descent of the River Sella has been declared an Event of International Tourist Interest.

In 1929, Dionisio de la Huerta, a few days before catching a train from Barcelona to Madrid, where he would take another to Asturias to spend the summer at his home in Coya (Infiesto), saw a folding canoe in the El Siglo department store. He bought it, and after arriving at his house in Asturias, he persuaded two of his friends, Doctor Benigno Morán and Manés Fernández, to canoe along the Piloña river from Coya to Infiesto, a distance of about 5 km that took them two and a half hours. This was the origin of what is now the descent of the River Sella. During the first official event in 1930, the participants reached Arriondas, and the following year Ribadesella. In 1932, the start and finish lines were finally established in Arriondas and Ribadesella, respectively. The descent started to be known all

Start in Arriondas

Finish in Ribadesella

Part of the descent

over Spain in 1935, with the participation of canoeists from outside Asturias. The 1936-1939 Civil War led the event to be suspended from 1936 to 1943. The first European canoeists entered in 1951, and the descent became an international event.

The descent starts at noon in Arriondas, with the participants and their canoes on land in their allocated positions. The finish line is beneath the Ribadesella bridge, 20 km from the start. The control closes 30 minutes after the winner reaches the finish line. Fans can follow the descent from what is called the "river train'.

APRIL FAIR

In April or May Seville celebrates its most colourful and lively fair, which is one of the most international festivals in Spain.

The April Fair, or Seville Fair, began in the mid-19th century as part of a livestock market held in the city. Paradoxically, the idea of the fair came from two people who lived in Seville but were originally from the Basque Country and Catalonia: José María Ybarra (1816-1878), a shipowner whose family founded Altos Hornos de Vizcaya, and Narciso Bonaplata (1807-1869), a Barcelona-born businessman in the textile sector, the owner of the El Vapor factory. The first *casetas* or booths, built to protect the animals from the heat of the sun, soon become small taverns that sold wine and cold cuts, and there was always a guitarist and someone would start to sing. The first official April Fair was inaugurated on 18th April 1847 in Prado de San Sebastián, as Queen Isabella II granted Seville a "fair" privilege. At that time Prado de San Sebastián was outside the city walls, but it is now in the centre, near the Tobacco Factory (University of Seville). The development of rail and road transport meant that livestock fairs became less important, but the fair held in Seville in April or May persisted as a place of entertainment.

Girls dressed in flamenco dresses at the April Fair

Officially, the fair starts at midnight on Monday when they "test the lights", in other words turn on thousands of lights that are particularly impressive at the main gate (50 m high). The fair, which currently takes place in the Los Remedios district, houses innumerable *casetas* decorated with flowers, streamers and lanterns. These *casetas* are like an extension of the home, and welcome friends, relatives and other guests with typical beverages and food. This warm and festive atmosphere is also found outside, and people usually dance in the streets which, for this occasion, are covered in *albero*, a kind of red sand, to prevent the horses from slipping. At night, in the

The lights are switched on

Carriage drivers

gleam of thousands of light bulbs, the *casetas* come to life with tapas, Andalusian white wine (*fino*, *moriles* or *manzanilla*) and *sevillanas* danced by men and women in traditional costume. The morning is the time of horses and their riders, and visitors can see different types of carriages and breeds of horse. The most popular carriages are called "charras", with just one seat, and "jardineras", used in the past to take bullfighters and their teams to the bullring.

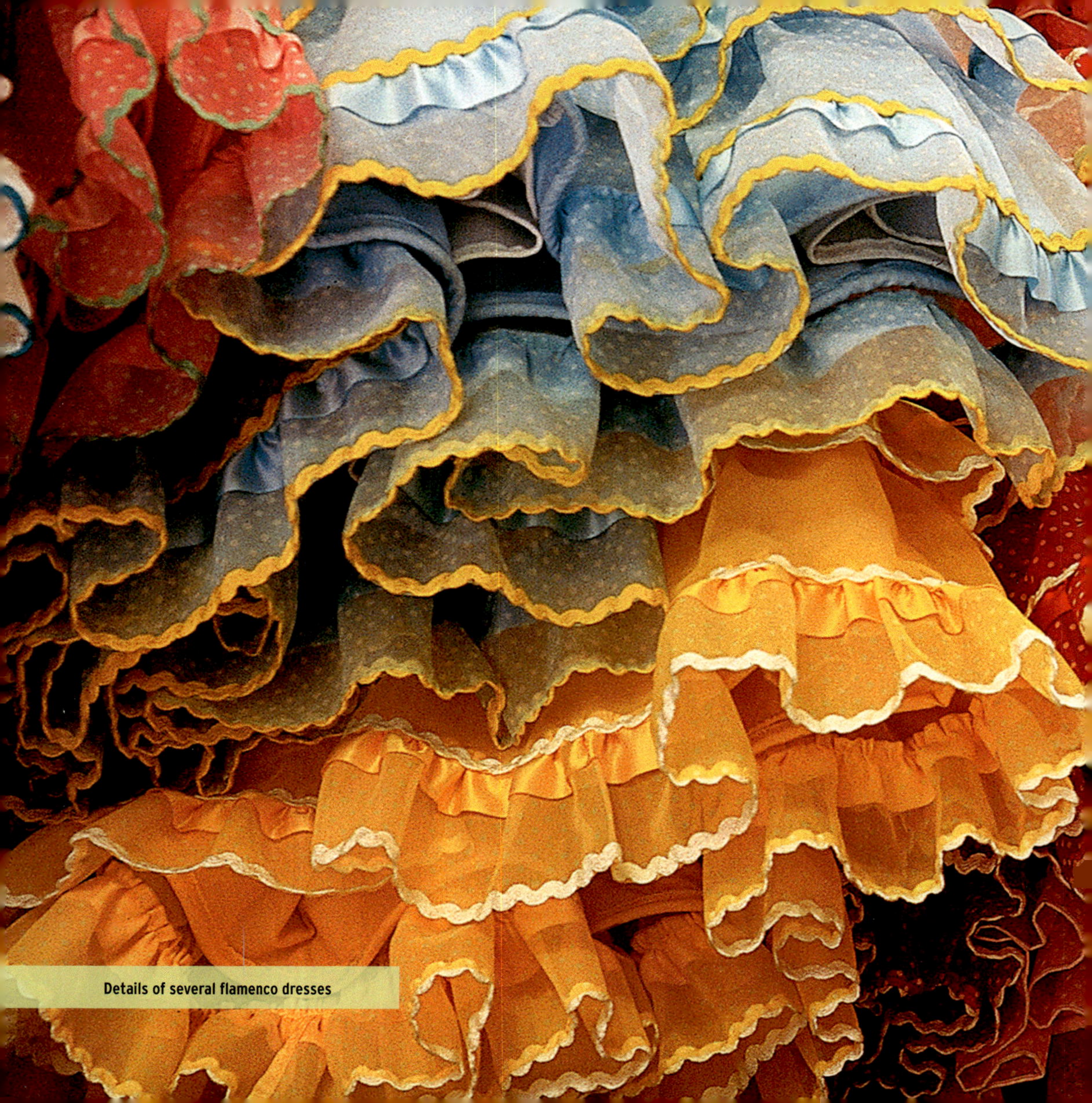

Details of several flamenco dresses

FLAMENCO AND *SEVILLANAS*

The first reports about flamenco, at least as it is conceived today, date from the last quarter of the 18th century. Its origins and historic evolution, however, are unknown. Felipe Pedrell (1841-1922), a well-known composer and musician born in Tortosa, in *Estudios sobre el folklore musical* maintains that flamenco song and dance contain traces of the origin of gypsies which numerous historians locate in Egypt. These eastern roots can be seen when comparing some particular aspects of flamenco song and dance with other music of Tunisian origin.

Flamenco comprises three fundamental factors: song, dance and guitar music. There are numerous flamenco song variants such as *malagueñas*, *milongas*, *bulerías*, *fandangos*, *sevillanas*, *siguiriyas*, etc. The dance comprises different sections: *llamada* (warning signal for the singer and guitarist), *escobilla* (part of dance with foot movements and sound), *cierre* (conclusion to a sequence of movements with heavy percussion and highly defined postures), *desplante* (final posture of a step), *remate* (emphasising the fall of the song),

Flamenco dancers

Dancer

paseo (steps for movement), *mudanza* (body movements without feet movements) and *toque*, or guitar accompaniment. Women dance flamenco in traditional costume, which was originally a simple dress with frills. This primitive costume evolved, and now involves a tight body down to the hip and a skirt with frills. After the 1990s, flamenco dresses lost their baroque embellishments and became lightweight, sensual attire.

Sevillanas, the typical songs and dances of Seville and its surrounding districts, are derived from the *seguidillas* of Castile and La Mancha, and they are sung and danced during popular events. The origin of *sevillanas* dates from the 14th century, from compositions known as "seguidillas castellanas" which, over time, evolved and took on flamenco rhythms. They were danced in the 18th century and gradually evolved to what they are today. *Sevillanas* are the most popular Spanish regional dance in the rest of the world.

Flamenco group

HORSE FAIR

Jerez de la Frontera holds its popular Horse Fair in May; it is an equestrian event of international renown.

The Horse Fair, which has been held since the 15th century, became as it is today when in 1903 the traditional livestock fair was combined with another popular fair by the inhabitants of Jerez de la Frontera. A document dated 13th September 1481 mentions a fair located in the same place. For most of the 20th century, the Horse Fair and the Wine Harvest Fair were the two most important events for the town, and its wineries, the "cathedrals of wine", opened their doors so that visitors could admire their cellars full of ancient wine casks. During the Horse Fair, which is visited by livestock breeders from the world over to buy pure bred horses, the horses are paraded by their riders and a large number of carriages drive through the fairground, adding colour and tradition.

Carriage contest

Participants in the Fair

The fair is held in González Hontoria park, which alternates *albero*, a kind of red sand, with flowerbeds and gardens. More than 250 *casetas* or booths are set up during the fair, each with its own atmosphere and its culinary specialities (fried *pescaíto* fish, oxtail, *tagarninas esparragás* made using the Spanish oyster thistle, tripe, *berza jerezana* stew, seafood, cold cuts, etc.), which compete for the prize for the best tapa and the best decor. Wine from Jerez, particularly *oloroso* and *fino*, is drunk in the *casetas*, nearly always with soda (known as *rebujitos*). If the participants are men and ride, they usually wear traditional costume in dark colours (grey, brown or black) while women wear gypsy or flamenco dresses with polka dots and frills. The fair starts when the light bulbs that comprise the gate to the fair and decorate its streets are switched on; every year they follow a different design.

COURTYARD FESTIVAL

This contest, which is held in the capital of the province of Cordoba, means visitors can see the courtyards of many private houses that are closed during the rest of the year.

This festival is of recent origin. The first dates back to 1912, and it had become very popular among locals by 1927. The contest began in 1933, and the first time there were 16 entries. The festival was again organised in 1943, since when it has grown in popularity and become an attraction for visitors to the city with more than a million coming each year. In 2012, the courtyards of Cordoba were declared Intangible Cultural Heritage of Humanity.

There are two types of courtyard in Cordoba: those that belong to individual houses, made of paving stones or mosaic and with the different rooms around them, and those that belong to blocks of houses and provide access to the individual dwellings. In the courtyards, the balcony railings are full of plant pots with many kinds of flowers, although geraniums

Courtyard in Cordoba

Colourful geraniums

are the most common. For a visit to the courtyards, we recommend going to the Alcázar Viejo district, between the Alcázar and St. Basil's Church, but there are also marvellous courtyards in the Santa María district, around San Lorenzo and the Magdalena. There are also samples of this culture in the old Jewish quarter around Cordoba's popular mosque. The best example, however, is in the Viana Palace (14th century), which is a Historic-Artistic Monument and Artistic Garden with its twelve different courtyards.

The courtyards that participate in the festival are divided into two categories: ancient and modern. During the contest, the City Council organises guided visits to show the beauty of popular Cordoban architecture. The festival is held with the collaboration of the San Benito District Residents' Association, which runs an open-air bar and dance by the Belén tower.

CHERRY BLOSSOM FESTIVAL

In spring the Jerte Valley, a district in Extremadura comprising eleven municipalities, celebrates its Cherry Blossom Festival.

This festival is subject to weather constraints that can evidently make the cherry trees bloom sooner or later in the year. In full bloom, more than a million cherry trees provide a unique landscape that covers the sides of the valley with white. The cherry trees are in bloom for 12-14 days, and this event announces the future harvest, particularly of what are known as *picotas*, a type of cherry that only grows here; when picked, its stalk remains on the tree. These cherries, protected by a Designation of Origin, are highly appreciated for their great quality and are exported to Germany, France and the UK. The blooming of cherry trees is celebrated in many parts of the world, including Japan, and their blossoms are grouped together in tiny bunches.

Over the years, the Cherry Blossom Festival has become more popular and other events, particularly culinary ones, have been organised to cater for the

Cherry trees in bloom, Jerte valley

Cherry grove, Jerte valley

Picota cherries

needs of the thousands of visitors who come to this part of Cáceres. The valley's typical dishes include tomato soup, bread and milk-based *cana* soup, "revolcás" potatoes, *migas* and kid stew, accompanied by a *pitarra* wine (the name comes from the name of a small pottery bowl).

The first cherry blossoms are usually seen in the warmest part of the valley, in Navaconcejo, Valdastillas and Rebollar, spreading to the rest of the Jerte valley a few days later: Tornavacas, Jerte, Barrado and Casas del Castañar. Visitors have to travel to all the towns and villages in the Jerte Valley district to see the blossoms.

FESTIVAL OF THE PILLAR

The festivities dedicated to the Virgin of the Pillar, the patron of Zaragoza, are held the week of 12th October and last for around ten days.

This festival, which commemorates the appearance of the Virgin Mary before St. James the Apostle during his evangelisation of Hispania, has only been held in its current form since the 19th century. However, in 1723 there is evidence of celebrating the Day of the Pillar, involving religious services, Masses, sermons, processions and rosaries. In 1807, the declaration of the Day of the Pillar as a compulsory religious festival made devotion to the Virgin, and the festival, more popular. In 1873, during the First Republic, a parade was organised and escorted by the Municipal Police of Zaragoza.

Floral offering to Virgin of the Pillar

The central and most popular event is the floral offering to the Virgin. It was first organised in 1958, six years after members of the Zaragoza City Council visited Castelló de la Plana (Valencia). The mayor of Zaragoza and his team were so impressed by the floral offering to the Virgin of Lledó (patron of Castelló de la Plana) that they decided to organise a similar event. The offering begins first thing in the morning on 12th October and lasts all day. Thousands of people wearing typical Aragonese costume (this is essential for participating) take flowers to the Virgin of the Pillar, located in the centre of the main square on top of a huge pyramid. In 2009, for instance, 450,000 people took flowers and, as every year, hundreds of volunteers used them to weave a multi-coloured mantle for the Virgin. The mantle shows the cross of Lorraine, the symbol of the worldwide battle against tuberculosis since 1902. This tradition dates from 1960 when a patient admitted to the Zaragoza Tuberculosis Hospital, known to the locals as "El Cascajo", now Royo Villanova General Hospital, suggested to a councillor that the hospital should present the Virgin of the Pillar with a cross of Lorraine (a two-barred red cross) on behalf of the patients.

Virgin of the Pillar

BONFIRES OF ST. JOHN

The bonfires of St. John, which are lit on the night of 23rd June, form part of a tradition found all along the Mediterranean coast.

The bonfires on St. John's day come from ancient worship of the god Mithra and celebration of the summer solstice. With Christianity, this pagan rite of sun worship was Christianised, as occurred with the

Burning *ninots* (dolls) on the eve of St. John's Day in Alicante

St. John bonfire in Alicante

winter solstice (Christmas), and started to be held on the day of John the Baptist. Christian tradition celebrates St. John's Day six months before Christmas because, according to the Gospels, his mother Elisabeth was six months' pregnant when an angel told her that her cousin Mary would be the mother of the Messiah. According to Christian tradition, Zacharias, Elisabeth's husband and the father of John the Baptist, lit a bonfire to commemorate this fact. Bonfires were originally believed to purify and even today people believe that they will be free from evil if they jump over them.

After its Christianisation, the ancient rite became an agricultural festival and the peasants who lived on

Eve of St. John's Day, fireworks on the beach

the Mediterranean coast celebrated the longest day of the year (summer solstice) for their harvests and the shortest day to keep away evil.

As in many other cities, in Alicante the bonfires of the summer solstice persisted over the centuries and the custom travelled from the countryside to the cities. However, although it is ancient, the first reports about bonfires in Alicante on St. John's Day (*fogueres de Sant Joan*) date to 1822, when it was forbidden to light bonfires in the streets and set off bangers and rockets with a fine ranging from 20 to 100 reales. The mayor of Alicante banned bonfires every year, but the people turned a deaf ear. As with other deeply rooted popular festivals, the authorities were ignored and there were always bonfires on the eve of St. John's Day.

Bonfires are still lit in the streets and on the beaches of the Spanish towns on the Mediterranean coast, with dinner also included during the festival. In Catalonia, for instance, the eve of St John's Day is when people eat the typical *coca* flatbread, covered with dry fruit as a symbol of the earth's riches, and they also drink cava and usually go for a swim in the sea to purify themselves.

TOMATINA

This festival, which is held in Bunyol in Valencia, has become very popular all over the world in just a few years and it attracts people from distant countries.

There are many versions of the origins of "tomatina", but the best documented shows that it began in 1945. That year, Bunyol Square was full of young people watching the parade of giants and figures with large heads. Several of them decided to join the parade; they were asked to leave by the people organising it and it all ended in a fight. Nearby there was a greengrocer's, and several of the youngsters grabbed tomatoes from their display boxes and started to throw them. The police broke up the fight, and its participants were made to pay for the damage caused. This was the origin of the "tomatina" (held on the last Wednesday in August), which was repeated for a few years until it was forbidden by the authorities. In 1955, a "tomato's funeral" was organised, with a large tomato in a coffin. During the parade, a local band played a funeral march. However, the festival continued and the Town Council finally gave in and permitted the tomato fight, although it was never incident-free. The festival was consolidated on an international scale thanks to a documentary broadcast in 1983 on the *Informe Semanal* TV programme.

***Tomatina* in Bunyol**

The "tomatina" now has the Council's official support and attracts more than 45,000 people every year, from Spain and other countries, to participate in this peculiar "peaceful" battle that uses around 125 tonnes of tomatoes (around 150,000 in all) specially grown for the event in Xilxes (Castelló). After a firework goes off, and shouting "tomato" at the top of their voice, the participants start to throw juicy tomatoes, distributed for free by the Council, at each other.

Tomato battle

FALLAS

The unquestionable protagonist of fallas, *the most important festival in the Valencia region, is fire.*

According to one tradition, *fallas* originated in the bonfires lit by carpenters with pieces of leftover wood on the Day of St. Joseph, their patron saint. On the same day, they also burned the *parots* or the structures used to hang the oil lamps that gave them light at night. When spring arrived, the days became longer and there was no need for *parots*. According to this theory, *parots* were the origin of present-day *ninots* (dolls). However, the fact that the worship of fire, a symbol of the sun, is widespread throughout the Mediterranean suggests a much more ancient origin, related to the worship of Mithra, the Persian god of the sun adapted to the Roman Empire, and agricultural rites related to spring and the first harvests. Like other traditions, rites and cults related to the sun were Christianised and assimilated by the new religion.

Floral offering

The first document that refers to *fallas* dates from 1740. There were already references to satirical monuments that were exhibited to bring public shame on people, often neighbours who had done something wrong during the year. In 1784, a municipal regulation forbid "the burning of *fallas*" in the city's narrowest streets. Gradually, the *fallas* of Valencia became more and more popular and other neighbouring towns, such as Alzira, Gandia and Xàtiva, also started to burn them.

In 1895, when prizes were created for the best *fallas*, they ended up with the master *falleros* who spent a lot of money over the course of the year to create the *ninots* that are to be burned. Together with fire another important aspect is the fireworks that have become essential in these festivities, each day of which starts with a *mascletà*, a roar of gunpowder and pyrotechnics.

***Falla* ready to be burnt**

Burning a *falla*

Nowadays *fallas* are satirical monuments that represent famous people (*ninots*), including politicians and celebrities, created with great skill by *fallero* artisans. A *falla* usually consists of a central figure or composition several metres high (as much as 30 m), surrounded by figures made from cardboard and expanded polystyrene. Around 400 *fallas* are erected in Valencia during the festivities, plus more than 200 in the rest of the province; they are visited by a million people.

FESTIVAL OF MOORS AND CHRISTIANS

These festivities, which are very popular in the Valencia region, commemorate ancient medieval battles between Muslims (Moors) and Christians.

Alcoi's festival of Moors and Christians commemorates the latter's victory at the battle of Alcoy which, according to tradition, involved locals fighting the army of Al-Azraq (1208-1276), a Muslim leader, son of a Christian mother, who lived in the ancient Kingdom of Valencia. According to legend, St. George appeared on the city walls to fight alongside the Christians in this battle. St. George is therefore the patron of the festivities held in his honour on 23rd April.

The first references to the Moors and Christians festival date from 1511, when documents refer to a "simulation of battle" and a festival in honour of St. George. The use of arquebuses and pikes was added to the festival in 1552. However, the most explicit document about it dates from 1672 and describes

Escuadra Contrabandistas (Christians)

Escuadra Alférez Benimerines (Moors)

Escuadra Alférez Cides (Christians)

the celebrations in honour of St. George and events to commemorate the expulsion of the Moors, with the participation of two singing groups, one of Moors and one of Christians.

The central part of the festival takes place on 23rd and 24th April. On the 23rd, at noon, a procession carries the relic of St. George from the Church of the same name to St. Mary's Church. The most emotional moment is in San Lorenzo Street, when people throw red and white rose petals as the Saint passes.

EL ROCÍO PILGRIMAGE

The Rocío pilgrimage, one of the most popular religious events of Andalusia, is to the Virgin of the same name as the village of El Rocío.

The Rocío pilgrimage is celebrated with great fervour on the weekend of Whit Sunday. The pilgrims leave on foot, on horseback, or in richly embellished carriages, surrounded by dance and song, to travel to the chapel of the Virgin of Rocío. Part of the route crosses the Doñana Nature Park and it has a considerable environmental impact on a unique European ecosystem.

The legend of the Virgin of Rocío dates from the 15th century. A hunter or livestock breeder, named by some sources as Gregorio Medina, from Villamanrique de la Condesa heard his dogs barking and indicating an impenetrable point of the marshes. He made his way among bushes and stagnant water to discover a full size image of the Virgin on the trunk of a tree. He took the image, intending to carry it to the

Church of Our Lady of Rocío

Procession of the Virgin of Rocío

village of Almonte, and left the marshes, but the image was so heavy and he became so tired that he fell asleep. When he woke up the Virgin had disappeared. He returned to where he had found it and there it was again. He went to Almonte, told everyone what had happened, and a group led by the priest decided to go to the marshes. The Virgin was there, on the same tree, and they took it to be a sign. They took the image to Almonte and soon afterwards started to build a chapel in the marsh so that the Virgin could stay where she had been found.

When they arrive at the chapel (the current building dates from the 16th century), the pilgrims wait for nightfall on Whit Sunday for what is known as the "salto de la reja" (jumping the railing). After praying a rosary, which starts at midnight, and the procession of *simpecados* or banners of the Virgin, the pilgrims literally jump the railing in front of the Virgin, who they call the "White Dove", and carry her in procession around the village. The procession visits the different brotherhoods and priests pray the *Salve*, accompanied by the pilgrims.

SANFERMINES

***The sanfermines, Spain's most international festival, are popular abroad thanks to novelist Ernest Hemingway and his book entitled* The Sun Also Rises.**

The festivities in honour of St. Fermín, the patron saint of Navarre (the patron saint of Pamplona is St. Saturnin), attract more than a million people every year. The origins of this festival are found in the Middle Ages, in a livestock fair. The *sanfermines* begin with the *chupinazo* rocket (6th July at noon) and end (14th July at midnight) with the traditional *Pobre de mí*, a farewell song.

The festivities are centred on the running of the bulls, where people run, followed by fighting bulls, the 849 metres that separate the Santo Domingo stables from the bullring. These *encierros* or races start at 8 in the morning, after a firework is set off, and many groups from Pamplona take part.

Bull running

Firing the chupinazo

VERBENA DE LA PALOMA

The* verbena *(street party) in honour of the Virgin of Paloma is an occasion to see some of the streets of Madrid finely decorated and in particular* chulos *and* chulapas, *traditional Madrid working-class people.

The "Verbena de la Paloma" (15th August) is held between 6th and 15th August around the Church of St. Peter the Royal, popularly known as the *Paloma* (dove or pigeon), a Neo-Mudéjar building that contains a painting of the *Virgen de la Paloma* that was discovered in a nearby courtyard (18th century). According to a report written in 1791 by the Marquis of Casa García Postigo, the canvas, which actually represents the Our Lady of Solitude, appeared in a courtyard and was given to some children to play with. Andrea Isabel Tintero, who lived in La Paloma Street, recovered the canvas, framed it and exhibited it by the door to her house. The image started to be venerated by the neighbours and this gradually spread to the rest of Madrid. So famous did the picture become that a chapel was built in 1796, which was later enlarged and became the current church in 1891. In the mid-20th century, the *verbena* lost popularity and only a few of the neighbours maintained it, due to tradition and nostalgia. However, in the 1980s the *verbena* recovered its appeal and became one of the most traditional festivals of Madrid.

Festival of the Virgin of Paloma

During the *verbena*, the streets are decorated to honour the Virgin, and *casetas* or booths are set up from Gran Vía de San Francisco and Carrera de San Francisco to Las Vistillas. Thousands of people from Madrid visit them in the evening; they dance and have fun while traditional *churros* or fritters are made. The popularity of this festival in the 19th century was reflected in the zarzuela entitled *La verbena de la Paloma*, by Tomás Bretón and Ricardo de la Vega.

The central act of the festival is when the painting of the Virgin is taken down by Madrid fire fighters who then take it to a float ready for the procession. The

***Chulapos* and *chulapas* in Puerta del Sol**

parade leaves the Church of St Peter the Royal and proceeds through the streets to the Church of St. Francis the Great, where it turns around and goes up Calatrava Street to take the Virgin back to her sanctuary. Back in the Church, the fire fighters return the painting to the altarpiece of the presbytery while the *Salve* is sung. The painting of the Virgin used to be placed on a float belonging to the Sacramental Brotherhood of St. Isidore, but in 1939 it was replaced by a fire engine decorated with typical Manila shawls.

Tapas in St. Michael's market

CUSTOMS AND TRADITIONS

TAPAS

The word "tapa" comes from the ancient custom of "tapar" (covering) glasses of wine to prevent flies or mosquitoes from falling into them.

Going for tapas, a typical custom only found in Spain, consists of eating small snacks in a bar while chatting with friends. These tapas, which are usually served together with a drink, are of ancient origin, although the first mention of the word "tapa" was not until 1939. According to one tradition, King Alfonso X the Wise of Spain, with a view to preventing people from getting drunk, ordered that bars in Castile should always serve something to eat with wine. At the time, tapas consisted of slices of ham, chorizo or cheese, which were placed on the top of the wine glass to comply with the royal order, and also prevent flies or other insects from falling into the wine.

Francisco de Quevedo, in *La vida del Buscón*, calls tapas "avisos" or "avisillos", food that accompanied

Casa Labra, Madrid

Casa Alberto, Madrid

wine before the main meal, nearly always while standing and chatting to friends. Another tradition maintains that tapas originated during the reign of Alfonso XIII of Spain. According to this hypothesis, the King was visiting the province of Cadiz and stopped for refreshments in the famous "Venta del Chato" (still open to the public as a restaurant). The monarch asked for a glass of sherry, it was served and a little later a breeze arose that moved the curtains. To prevent the sand from the beach entering the King's wine, the owner of the tavern placed a slice of ham over his glass. The King thought that it was a great idea. He drank the sherry, ate the ham and asked for another glass with the same tapa.

However, culinary historians believe that tapas are more ancient, and could even be associated with the Arabic custom of serving several dishes in small portions.

Tapas have now evolved considerably to become culinary specialities that characterise many bars and restaurants. In Andalusia, Madrid and the Basque Country, tapas acquire a special dimension: they include everything from croquettes, fried or battered squid, omelettes, peppers, olives and anchovies in vinegar to other more complex snacks such as *tostas* (slices of toasted bread with cold cuts) of roast and marinated ham with cheese, pork cooked in caramel or courgette rolls stuffed with spinach and goat's cheese.

Dish of tapas

BULLFIGHTS

Bullfights, with bullfighters on foot or on horseback (rejoneo) take place in Spain, Portugal, the south of France and South America.

Bullfights originated in the Graeco-Latin fights that took root in Roman Hispania. The cult and ritual slaughter of bulls became of great importance in the Mediterranean basin, especially in the civilisation of Crete, as shown by the frescos in Knossos palace.

At bullfights, the bullfighters wear the well-known *traje de luces* (suit of lights, so called because of how they are decorated), which dates from the 18th century. Before then, they wore a *traje de majo*, associated with the *majista* movement that supported the popular traditions of Madrid against the fashion of the court. Bullfighting techniques and styles are constantly evolving, and bullfighters now tend to move around much more in contrast to the traditional style of staying still.

Half *verónica* pass

Bullfights begin at a signal of the president (the authority who ensures order in the ring), consisting of waving a white handkerchief. Music of bugles and drums accompanies the entry parade led by the *alguaciles* (responsible for implementing the president's orders) followed by the bullfighters, or *espadas* (as they kill the bulls with a sword), in order of seniority, the *cuadrillas* (members of each bullfighter's team), the *picadores* (fighters on horseback who prepare the bulls for the fight using a long pike) and the *peones* (who help the bullfighter).

Bullfighter's jacket and cape

Blood coloured jacket with gold embroidery

They halt in front of the president to salute the authorities and then, with the ring in complete silence, the *toriles* door opens and the first of six bulls enters the ring.

The bullfighter whose bull has been released uses a cape to see how "brave" the animal is and decide on how to proceed. After a few swishes of the cape the president then waves his white handkerchief again to authorise the entry of the *picadores*, who use their long pike to make several *puyas* (name of the end of the pike fitted with a three-bladed iron tip) to reduce the bull's strength in what is known as the "tercio de varas".

The president's handkerchief again announces a change of *tercio* (stage of the bullfight) and the *banderilleros* attract the attention of the bull and wait for it on foot before they stick up to three pairs of *banderillas* in its back. Bugles and trumpets announce the final "tercio de muleta" or "of death". The bullfighter then usually dedicates the bull to either a person in the audience or to the public. In this final part, the bullfighter controls the bull, showing his mastery. When the bull "squares up", meaning that its feet are squared and it is standing straight, the bullfighter attempts to push his sword into what is called the "hoyo de las agujas" to cleanly kill the bull.

***Lance de revolera* on knees**

After the fight, the public decides how good the fighter has been, with applause for good fights or whistles and booing for bad ones. The president only awards the bullfighter one of the bull's ears if the public waves white handkerchiefs for a few minutes. If the fight was very good, the public applauds and

Lance de chicuelina

Banderillero

encourage the bullfighter to go on a lap of honour around the bullring. If the president awards the fighter a second ear, he can "be carried out of the main door on the public's shoulders", a distinction that is highly appreciated by bullfighters in all important bullrings. Bullfights usually last two and a half hours.

Bullfighters who for whatever reason give up bullfighting go through the ritual of "cutting off their pigtail", which nowadays is not real hair but rather a hairpiece.

***Alguaciles* (mounted officials)**

HOLY WEEK

Primarily in Andalusia and Castile, Holy Week has a special dimension due to their majestic floats and the fervour of the brethren.

The origins of Holy Week date back to the start of Christianity, as shown by the fact that it is referred to by St. Eusebius as *heddomada vigiliarum* ("week of vigil"). However, the Holy Week processions of Seville, the most famous in Spain, are only documented from the 16th century. The first route for the Seville processions, dating from 1520, goes from the chapel of Casa de Pilatos to the Mudéjar shrine of El Campo. This Stations of the Cross parade became so well known that it was painted by Velázquez in the 17th century. There are some differences between Holy Week in Andalusia and Holy Week in Castile. The former is much more spectacular, with richly embellished floats featuring silver and gold poles, images with sorrowful faces, lanterns and garlands, while Holy Week in Castile is much more austere, and is practically an expression of grief in itself.

There are processions every day in Holy Week, with the participation of different brotherhoods. The floats used in Holy Week are called *pasos*, and they are carried on the shoulders of groups of men called *costaleros*. With their sculpted or dressed images, the different *pasos* represent the passion of Christ at

Holy Week, Seville

Brethren and St. Elisabeth's Church, Zaragoza

Costaleros, Seville

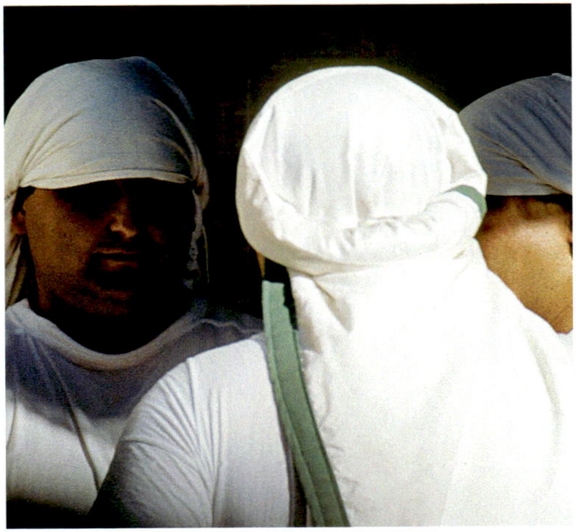

Calvary. Most of the *pasos* carry images of the Virgin Mary, enthroned as the "queen of grief" because of her Son's death. In general, these figures date from the 17th or 18th century, when great sculptors were working in Andalusia and Castile. The most famous include Martínez Montañés, Juan de Mesa, Ruiz Gijón and La Roldana. The processions are usually led by the *mulidor*, who dresses in ancient costume and rings a bell to announce the brotherhood's arrival. The procession proper is opened by the "guiding cross". It is followed by Nazarenes or penitents, who wear *capirotes*, cone-shaped headwear that was used by those who were condemned by the Inquisition, together with long tunics. In some brotherhoods, penitents drag along chains that are secured to their ankles, while carrying large candles in their hands. There are people responsible for steering the *pasos*, and they give instructions to the *costaleros*. The *capataz* is the person in charge of everything and he is usually accompanied by an assistant. The processions are followed by bands playing music. Some images, for instance the *Cristo de la Buena Muerte* (Christ of the Good Death) in Malaga, are escorted by the Spanish Foreign Legion. However, each brotherhood

Nazarenes, Seville

Brethren and the wall of La Parroquieta, Zaragoza

has its own organisation and both the processions and the *pasos* differ considerably from one region to another. People line streets and squares to watch the processions and the *pasos*, primarily at the doors of their churches, when the *costaleros* have to use all their skills to bring the images out or return them to their places. *Saetas* are often sung as the *pasos* proceed in Andalusia.

Entombment of Christ, Bercianos de Aliste

Some brotherhoods are enormously popular in Spain. This is the case of Jesús del Gran Poder (Seville), established in 1431 by the Dukes of Medinaceli in the Santo Domingo de Silos monastery (now the parish church of St. Benedict). The brotherhood of the Empalaos comes from Valverde de la Vera (Cáceres) and its penitents have ropes wound around their chests and carry a heavy piece of wood weighed down with iron rings tied to their arms outstretched in a crucifix position. Finally, as an example of the diversity of Holy Week events in Spain, in The Entombment of Christ procession in Bercianos de Aliste (Zamora) the penitents wear their shrouds in a process that recreates Christ's Descent from the Cross.

WAY OF ST. JAMES

Pilgrimages to Santiago de Compostela became popular after King Alfonso II the Pure visited the tomb to pay tribute to the apostle.

Scallop shell with St. James's cross

The discovery of what is assumed to be the tomb of the apostle St. James (Santiago) (9th century) in Galicia, signalled the beginning of a pilgrimage that is very much alive today and is internationally famous. Although most modern studies rule out the evangelisation of Spain by St. James, an ancient tradition argues that the apostle sailed from Jerusalem to the port of Iria (A Coruña) to spread the gospel in Roman Hispania. According to legend, after St. James's decapitation in Jerusalem, his body was brought by his disciples to Spain and, after numerous problems, buried on a piece of land provided by Queen Lupa. In 813, when the legend of St. James's evangelisation was consolidated in Spain, a hermit called Pelayo was at the entrance to his cave when he saw some strange lights over a hill, crowned by a fortification. The hermit, convinced that the lights

Map of the French Way

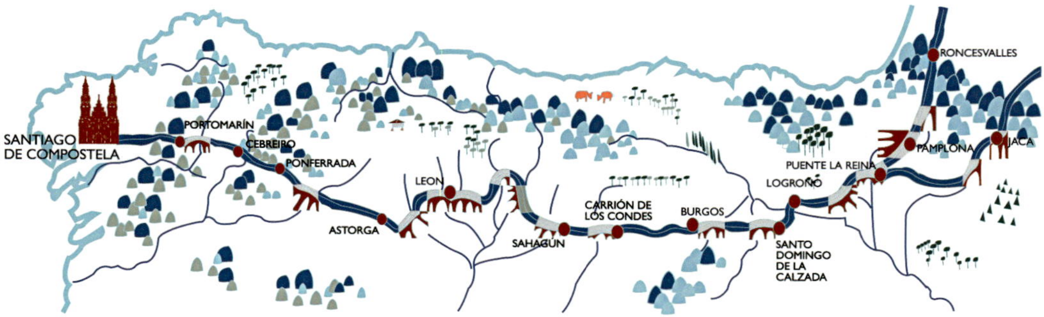

Itero del Castillo bridge, Burgos

St. James the Apostle (16th century)

were the will of the Lord, decided to tell the bishop, Teodomiro de Iria Flavia, who visited the hill and also saw the lights. After fasting for several days, the bishop decided to dig and he discovered what was assumed to be St. James's tomb.

This discovery attracted pilgrims to the tomb and their number gradually increased and became enormous by the Middle Ages. The pilgrimage of King Alfonso II the Pure of Spain also made the first pilgrimages popular and a city gradually rose around the tomb, which over the centuries became known as Santiago de Compostela. A martyrology (c. 867), drafted by Usardo, a monk from the Saint

Astorga Cathedral, León

Germain-des-Prés (Paris) monastery, says that, in Spain "the sacred bones of St. James are the object of special veneration", showing the importance of the pilgrimages to the apostle's tomb and that they were famous abroad as early as the 9th century.

The flow of pilgrims ceased in the 10th century after the conquest of Compostela by Almanzor, although the Way of St. James was subsequently recovered by the Cluny monks. At the end of the 12th century, the Order of Santiago, established in Cáceres (1170) during the reign of King Ferdinand II of León, became responsible for protecting all pilgrims travelling to Compostela. The Way began to decline in the 14th century due to the black death that spread over Europe and killed around 25 million people. Later on, in the 16th century, the Protestant Reformation and Philip II of Spain's fear that it would spread to his

Monastery of St. Clare, Carrión de los Condes, Palencia

Pilgrims on Monte do Gozo, Santiago de Compostela

country led to restrictions on the pilgrims. Thanks to an initiative of the Galicia Regional Government, the Way of St. James recovered all its splendour in 1993.

THE THREE KINGS AND PARADE

The Kings and their parades in all the cities and towns of Spain are the most important children's festival of the year.

The three Kings are called Melchior, Caspar and Balthazar and, according to Christian tradition, they visited Jesus when he was born, guided by a star. They gave him three highly symbolic gifts: gold, frankincense and myrrh.

Some sacred texts that are not in either the Old or New Testament, such as the Gospel of Thomas (2nd century), provide more details about these mysterious characters. This gospel, classified as apocryphal by the Church, tells that the three Kings were indeed related, and that they arrived in Bethlehem escorted by three legions of soldiers from Persia, Babylon and Asia, respectively.

According to the tradition followed in Spain, Melchior was an old European with white hair and beard, and his gift was myrrh, an oil used for anointing. Caspar, the youngest and blondest of the three, came from Asia and brought an aromatic resin with him, frankincense. Finally, Balthazar was black, came from Africa and brought gold, the most precious of all metals.

On 5th January, Spanish children are visited by the Kings, who bring them the presents that they have asked for in letters they give to the royal postmen. They have to have behaved well throughout the year as the Kings know exactly how good they have been. If they have not behaved well, they do not get any presents and are left instead with a sweet that looks like coal (in Catalonia the sweet looks like a turd). So

Fireworks during the parade

Parade of the Kings in Madrid

that the Kings know where they live, children leave their shoes out to make sure that each present will be left in the right place.

In some countries, children do not send their letters but leave them inside their shoes.

Children also leave food out for the camels that are used by the Kings to carry their presents. Typically this is a bowl of water and some stale bread or dry grass. Next to the shoes they also put food for the Kings, such as pastries or nougat, together with three glasses of water.

NEW YEAR'S GRAPES

It is traditional in Spain to eat twelve grapes as the clock strikes midnight on New Year's Eve for good luck.

The origins of this tradition are uncertain. According to some newspapers and magazines from the late 19th century, the custom of eating grapes on New Year's Eve originated in France. On 2nd January 1894, *El Siglo Futuro* magazine included an article that had previously been published in the *El Imparcial* newspaper, entitled "lucky grapes", which said that "[This custom], imported from France, has become second nature to us". In France, well-off families used to eat grapes and drink champagne. To make fun of them, a group of people from Madrid decided to go to the Puerta del Sol on New Year's Eve to eat twelve grapes as the clock struck twelve. In 1895, the press in Madrid also referred to the custom of eating "lucky grapes": "It is custom in Madrid," said an evening paper, "to eat twelve grapes as the clock strikes twelve to signal the new year." The tradition of eating grapes at Puerta del Sol took root and soon spread all over Spain, and they were also eaten in Tenerife by 1903.

Twelve lucky grapes

Another theory, endorsed by leading historians, claims that there was a bumper crop of grapes in Almeria, Alicante and Murcia in 1909, and the tradition of eating twelve grapes was promoted as a marketing strategy. In 1962, Spanish television started to broadcast the clock in Puerta del Sol striking midnight on New Year's eve, and it has become such a staple event that millions of people watch it each year. The custom soon became popular in some South American countries, and twelve grapes are now eaten in Mexico, Venezuela, Bolivia, Argentina and Chile.

Although eating twelve grapes on New Year's Eve is a relatively modern custom, in ancient times grapes and vines were very symbolic, mainly in the Christian world. Wine was also considered to be the image of knowledge. Nowadays the twelve grapes eaten on New Year's Eve are associated with abundance, and according to tradition you should make a wish when you eat each one.

New Year's Eve at Puerta del Sol

SIESTA

The siesta, a Spanish custom that consists of napping after lunch, is designed to recover energy for the rest of the day.

The siesta (or afternoon nap) is not only a Spanish custom as it is found in many South American, Middle Eastern and African countries, plus China, Taiwan, the Philippines, India, Italy, Greece and France. The word "siesta" comes from the Latin *sexta*, the sixth hour of the day, midday according to solar time (2 p.m.), when Romans used to rest.

Experts claim that the siesta became rooted in Spain because of two decisive factors. The first is the natural drowsiness that occurs after meals, when the flow of blood to the nervous system is reduced as it increases to the stomach; the second is the fact that Spanish lunches tend to be long and heavy compared to other countries. In many European countries, for instance, the biggest meal is breakfast to meet the body's requirements for the day.

***The siesta,* Vincent van Gogh**

Also, in many warm or hot countries, the siesta usually coincides with the hottest part of the day. A siesta of about thirty minutes is considered to be very beneficial for health, and people such as Albert Einstein, who visited Spain, and Winston Churchill, who got used to the siesta in Cuba, were supporters of the custom. For Camilo José Cela, who won the Nobel Prize for Literature in 1989, the siesta should be "with pyjamas, Our Father and a chamber pot". Miguel de Cervantes, in his novel entitled *The Ingenious Gentleman Don Quixote of La Mancha*, also refers to the siesta: "They came upon a field of fresh grass, where they spent the hours of the siesta, which was just beginning". Medical studies have shown that the siesta helps to increase productivity and reduce absenteeism and accidents at work, because people otherwise do not rest enough. Many specialists argue that the siesta is not a custom but a physiological necessity. Siestas protect against stress and prevent heart disease.

RATONCITO PÉREZ

According to tradition, when a child loses a milk tooth, they should put it under their pillow at night and Ratoncito Pérez (Little Mouse Pérez) will come for it and leave a few coins in its place.

This universal custom varies in different countries. In Italy it is known as Topolino, in France as *le Petite Souris* (*little mouse*) and in Britain as the Tooth Fairy. In Spain it also has different names, depending on the region: in Cantabria it is *L'Esquilu de los Dientis* (the tooth squirrel), in Catalonia *L'Angelet* (the little angel) and in the Basque Country *Maritxu Teilatukoa* (Mary from the Roof).

Cover of the tale

Plaque in Calle Arenal, 8 in Madrid

In Spain, the tradition took root thanks to Luis Coloma (1851-1915), a Jesuit, writer and journalist, the son of the famous Doctor Ramón Coloma. At the end of the 19th century, the secretary of Queen María Cristina of Habsburg, the regent after the death of her husband, Alfonso XI of Spain, until her son came of age, asked Luis Coloma to write a tale for the child who was then 8 and would become King Alfonso XIII. Father Coloma wrote the tale of *Ratoncito Pérez* , in which the protagonist was King Buby (the name Maria Christina used to refer to her son Alfonso) who left a tooth beneath his pillow and waited for the little mouse to come. The tale became very popular and spread from the court throughout the country. The mouse then became famous in South America, and children across half the world now wait for it whenever they lose a tooth.

© PHOTOGRAPHY CREDITS

We would like to acknowledge the collaboration of all entities and people who have made this edition possible.

Agencia de Viajes Tomatina.es, 270
Agrupación Castiza el Orgullo de Madrid, 280
Alfonso Suárez, 91a, 93
Archivo Fotográfico MNAR, Cover, 88, 89
ASF Imagen, 294b
Asociación Madrileña los Chulapos del Puente de Vallecas, 281
Ayuntamiento de Baiona, 185
Ayuntamiento de Catoira, 240
Ayuntamiento de Chinchón, 171a
Ayuntamiento de León, 58, 59
Ayuntamiento de Llanes, 144, 145
Ayuntamiento de Oviedo, 90
Ayuntamiento de Pamplona, 278, 279
Ayuntamiento de Sigüenza, 164, 165
Ayuntamiento de Trujillo, 150, 151
Beher, 227
Bodegas Hermanos Pérez Pascuas, 233b
Bodegas Martín Berdugo, 233d
Bodegas Tío Pepe, 234a
Bodegas Ysios, 233a
Carlos Jiménez Ruiz, 52a
Castellers de Barcelona - Àngels Goenaga, 248, 249
Chiyosi Sugawara-2006 MacPower, 84b
Comunicación Universidad de Salamanca, 100
Consejo Regulador DOP Pimentón de la Vera, 224b
Consejo Regulador IGP Alcachofa de Tudela, 225a
Consejo Regulador IGP Jijona y Turrón de Alicante, 222, 223
Consorcio Ciudad Monumental de Mérida - J.M. Romero, 86, 87
Consorcio de Turismo de Córdoba, 262, 263
CRIIGG Aguardientes y Licores Tradicionales de Galicia, 236, 237
Dehesa Maladua, 226
Descenso del Sella, 252
Ediciones Palacios y Museos, 35, 66, 67, 68, 69, 70, 155, 254, 255, 256, 272, 273, 284, 285a
Ediciones Palacios y Museos, Covadonga Noriega, 49, 180b, 181, 277, 290
Ediciones Palacios y Museos, Cristina Rivarola, 202, 205, 207, 209, 210, 211, 212, 214, 229b
Ediciones Palacios y Museos, Gastromedia, 213, 215
Ediciones Palacios y Museos, Hidalgo y Lopesinos, 50, 54
Ediciones Palacios y Museos, Ignasi Rovira, 38
Ediciones Palacios y Museos, Joaquín Matamales Zanón, 271
Ediciones Palacios y Museos, José Barea, 24, 26, 27, 28, 60, 61, 62, 63, 64, 71, 76, 77, 78, 79, 81, 104, 105, 106, 108, 109, 112, 113, 114, 128, 133, 134, 135, 182b, 183, 282
Ediciones Palacios y Museos, Miguel Ángel Nistral, 110
Ediciones Palacios y Museos, Mike Merchant, 30b, 31

Ediciones Palacios y Museos, Patrimonio Nacional, Ignasi Rovira, 97, 98, 99
Ediciones Palacios y Museos, Patrimonio Nacional, José Barea, 167, 169a, 172, 173, 174, 175, 176
EFE, Lavandeira jr, 21
Fondo Fotográfico Ayuntamiento de Almagro (Concejalía de Cultura), 161
Foto Aurora, 188, 189a
Freixenet, 233c
Fundación Cueva de Nerja, Pedro Garrido, 180a
Fundación Museo Sorolla, José Barea, 72, 73
Iberimage, 291b, 292a
Infoasturias, 91b
Infoasturias, José Suárez, 238, 239
Madrid Destino, 298, 299, 301
Manu López Iglesias, 260, 261
MEH (Museo de la Evolución Humana de Burgos), 12
Mercado de San Miguel, 82, 83
Mercado Fontán, 92
Muralla de Ávila, Rafael Delgado, 25
Museo Arqueológico Nacional - Santiago Relanzón, 13
Museo de Altamira, Bustamante Hurtado, 157
Museo de Altamira, Pedro Saura, 156
Museo del Greco, 127
Museo del Prado, 67, 131
Museo Picasso Málaga, Bleday Rosa, 85
Museo Picasso Málaga, David Heald, 84a
Museu Picasso Barcelona, Caterina Barjau, 34
Oficina de Turisme de Figueres, 162, 163
Oficina de Turismo de Bermeo, 198
Oficina Municipal de Turismo de Luarca, 147b
Patronato Costa Blanca, 268a
Patronato Municipal de Turismo de Toledo, Ayuntamiento de Toledo, Agustín Martínez, 122
Patronato Municipal de Turismo de Toledo, Ayuntamiento de Toledo, Agustín Puig, 123
Patronato Municipal de Turismo de Toledo, Ayuntamiento de Toledo, José Ramón Márquez, 126
Patronato Municipal de Turismo y Playas de Alicante, 269
Patronato Municipal de Turismo y Playas de Alicante, Marien Llorens, 268b
Patronato Provincial de Turismo de la Diputación de Cádiz, David Ibáñez Montañez, 250, 251
Real Maestranza de Caballería de Ronda, 288, 289
Real Maestranza de Caballería de Ronda, José Morón, 182a
Ricard Pla y Pere Vivas, 32
Sastrería Taurina Santos, 287a
Sucesión Pablo Picasso, VEGAP, Madrid 2014, 69
Tomás Domínguez, 189b
Touristinfo Alcoy, Paco Grau, 274, 275
Turisme de l'Escala, 230, 231
Turismo de Arcos de la Frontera, 152, 153
Turismo de Haro, 244, 245
Turismo de Lena, 94a
Turismo de Ribadesella, 253
Turismo de Salamanca, 101, 102, 103
Turismo de Sevilla, 116, 117a
Turismo de Sevilla, Antonio del Junco, 117b
Turismo de Tenerife, 246, 247b
Turismo de Tenerife, Jesús D'Sousa, 247a
Turismo Valle del Jerte, Ángel Vicente Simón, 264, 265a
Turisvalencia, 132
Yolanda Ruiz/Enric Balasch, 10, 14, 15, 19, 22, 30a, 33, 36, 37, 39, 40, 41, 42, 43, 44, 45, 46, 47, 48, 51, 52b, 53, 56, 57, 74, 75, 94b, 95, 96, 107, 111, 118, 119, 120, 121, 124, 125, 137, 138, 139, 140, 142, 143, 146, 147b, 148, 149, 154, 158, 159, 160, 166, 168, 169b, 170, 171b, 178, 179, 184, 186, 187, 190, 191, 194, 195, 196, 197, 199, 200, 201, 217, 219, 221, 224a, 228, 229a, 232, 234b, 235, 242, 243, 258, 259, 276, 285b, 287b, 293, 294a, 295, 296, 297, 300
Zaragoza Turismo, Agustín Martínez, 136, 267, 291a
Zaragoza Turismo, Aranzazu Peyrotau, 266
Zaragoza Turismo, Daniel Marcos, 292b